Freshwater Fish of

Florida

FIELD GUIDE

D1559350

by Dave Bosanko

Adventure Publications, Inc.
Cambridge, MN

Edited by Brett Ortler

Cover and book design by Jonathan Norberg

Illustration credits by artist and page number:

Cover illustrations: Largemouth Bass (main) and Bluegill (upper front cover and back cover) by Duane Raver/USFWS

MyFWC.com/fishing: 11 **Julie Martinez:** 24, 26, 44, 46, 48 (both), 50, 52, 54, 56, 58, 60, 64, 68, 116, 118, 132, 162 **Duane Raver/USFWS:** 10, 18, 28, 30, 32, 34, 36, 38, 40,62, 66, 70, 72, 74, 76, 80, 86, 92, 102, 112, 122 (both), 130, 134, 142, 144, 146, 148, 150, 154, 156, 160, 164, 166, 168 **Joseph Tomelleri:** 42 (both), 78, 82, 84, 88, 90 (both), 94, 96, 98, 100, 104, 106, 108, 110, 114, 120, 124, 126 (both), 128, 136, 138, 140, 152, 158, 170, 172

10 9 8 7 6 5 4 3 2 1

Copyright 2009 by Dave Bosanko
Published by Adventure Publications, Inc.
820 Cleveland St. S
Cambridge, MN 55008
1-800-678-7006
www.adventurepublications.net
Printed in China
ISBN-13: 978-1-59193-218-5
ISBN-10: 1-59193-218-1

TABLE OF CONTENTS

3

4

HOW TO USE THIS BOOK

Your *Fish of Florida Field Guide* is designed to make it easy to identify more than 80 species of the most common and important fish in Florida and learn fascinating facts about each species' range, natural history and more.

The fish are organized by families, such as Catfish (*Ictaluridae*), Perch (*Percidae*), and Sunfish (*Centrarchidae*), which are listed in alphabetical order. Within these families, individual species are arranged alphabetically in their appropriate groups. For example, members of the Sunfish family are divided into Black Bass, Crappie and True Sunfish groups. For a detailed list of fish families and individual species, turn to the Table of Contents (pp. 3-7); the Index (pp. 178-183) provides a reference guide to fish by common name (such as Lake Trout) and other common terms for the species.

Fish Identification

Determining a fish's body shape is the first step to identifying it. Each fish family usually exhibits one or sometimes two basic outlines. Catfish have long, stout bodies with flattened heads, barbels or "whiskers" around the mouth, a relatively tall but narrow dorsal fin and an adipose fin. There are two forms of Sunfish: the flat, round, plate-like outline we see in Bluegills, and the torpedo or "fusiform" shape of Largemouth Bass.

In this field guide you can quickly identify a fish by first matching its general body shape to one of the fish family silhouettes listed in the Table of Contents (pp. 3-7). From there, turn to that family's section and use the illustrations and text descriptions to identify your fish. Example Pages (pp. 22-23) are provided to explain how the information is presented in each two-page spread.

For some species, the illustration will be enough to identify your catch, but it is important to note that your fish may not look exactly like the artwork. Fish frequently change colors. Males that are brightly colored during the spawning season may exhibit muted coloration at other times. Likewise, bass caught in muddy streams show much less pattern than those taken from clear lakes—and all fish lose some of their markings and color when removed from the water.

Most fish are similar in appearance to one or more other species—often, but not always, within the same family. For example, the Suwannee Bass is remarkably similar to the Spotted Bass. To accurately identify such look-alikes, check the inset illustrations and accompanying notes below the main illustration, under the "Similar Species" heading.

Throughout Fish of Florida we use basic biological and fisheries management terms that refer to physical characteristics or conditions of fish and their environment, such as dorsal fin or turbid water. For your convenience, these are listed and defined in the Glossary (pp. 174-177), along with other handy fish-related terms and their definitions.

Understanding such terminology will help you make sense of reports on state and federal research, fish population surveys, lake assessments, management plans and other important fisheries documents.

FISH ANATOMY

It's much easier to identify fish if you know the names of different parts of a fish. For example, it's easier to use the term "adipose fin" to indicate the small, soft, fleshy flap on a Catfish's back than to try to describe it. The following illustrations point out the basic parts of a fish; the accompanying text defines these characteristics.

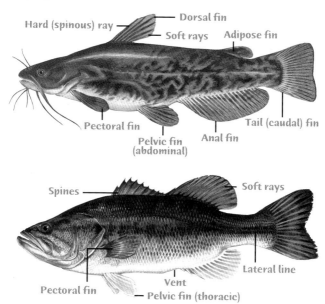

Fins are made up of bony structures that support a membrane. There are three kinds of bony structures in fins: **Soft rays** are flexible fin supports and are often branched.

Spines are stiff, often sharp, supports that are not jointed. **Hard rays** are stiff, pointed, barbed structures that can be raised or lowered. Catfish are famous for their hard rays, which are often mistakenly called spines. Sunfish have soft rays associated with spines to form a prominent dorsal fin.

Fins are named by their position on the fish. The **dorsal fin** is on top along the midline. A few species have another fin on their back, called an **adipose fin**. This small, fleshy protuberance located between the dorsal fin and the tail is distinctive of catfish, trout and salmon. **Pectoral fins** are found on each side of the fish near the gills. The **anal fin** is located along the midline, on the fish's bottom or *ventral* side. There is also a paired set of fins on the bottom of the fish, called the **pelvic fins**. These can be in the thoracic position (just below the pectoral fins) or farther back on the stomach, in the **abdominal position**. The tail is known as the **caudal fin**.

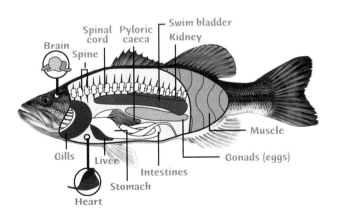

Eyes—A fish's eyes can detect color. Their eyes are rounder than those of mammals because of the refractive index of water; focus is achieved by moving the lens in and out, not by distorting light as is the case with mammals. Different species have varying levels of eyesight. Walleyes see well in low light. Bluegills have excellent daytime vision but see poorly at night, making them vulnerable to predation.

Nostrils—A pair of nostrils, or nares, is used to detect odors in the water. Eels and catfishes have a particularly well-developed sense of smell.

Mouth—The shape of the mouth is a clue to what the fish eats. The larger the food it consumes, the larger the mouth.

Teeth—Not all fish have teeth, but those that do have mouth gear designed to help them feed. Gars, Pickerels and Bowfins have sharp canine teeth for grabbing and holding prey. Minnows have *pharyngeal* teeth—located in the throat—for grinding.

Catfish have *cardiform* teeth, which feel like a rough patch in the front of the mouth. Bass have patches of *vomerine* teeth on the roof of their mouths.

Swim Bladder—Almost all fish have a swim bladder, a balloon-like organ that helps the fish regulate its buoyancy.

Lateral Line—This sensory organ helps the fish detect movement in the water (to help avoid predators or capture prey) as well as water currents and pressure changes. It consists of fluid-filled sacs with hair-like sensors, which are open to the water through a row of pores in their skin along each side—creating a visible line along the fish's side.

FISH NAMES

A Shellcracker is a Shellcracker in Florida, but in the northern parts of its range, Indianans call it a Redear Sunfish. In other regions, it's known as a stumpknocker or yellow bream.

Because common names may vary regionally, and even change for different sizes of the same species, scientific names are used that are exactly the same around the world. Each species has only one correct scientific name that can be recognized anywhere, in any language. The Largemouth Bass is *Micropterus salmoides* from Miami to Tokyo.

Scientific names are made up of Greek or Latin words that often describe the species. There are two parts to a scientific name: the generic or "genus," which is capitalized (*Micropterus*), and the specific name, which is not capitalized (*salmoides*). Both are always written in italic text or underlined.

A species' genus represents a group of closely related fish. The Largemouth and Suwannee Bass are in the same genus, so they share the generic name *Micropterus*. But each has a different specific name, *salmoides* for Largemouth Bass, *notius* for the Suwannee Bass.

ABOUT FLORIDA FISH

Florida is surrounded by salt water and covered by fresh water. In all, fresh water covers over 3 million acres of the state. This water takes many different forms; there are over 1,700 rivers and streams, 7,800 lakes and 600 clearwater springs, including temperate streams in the northwest, clear springs in north-central Florida, subtropical swamps in the south and tropical pools in the Keys.

Variety of habitat leads to a variety of species; of the 270 species that reside in Florida, just under 200 species are native, and about 70 were introduced by humans in the last 100 years.

This book covers over 70 fish species, and includes those someone spending time on Florida's lakes and streams is most likely to encounter. For most of these species, fresh water is their only home, though some species spend part of the year in salt water or in brackish water. The 30 or so species targeted by recreational fishermen are included, as are 40 additional species of particular interest, either because these species are baitfish, or because they have some unique or interesting characteristic.

FREQUENTLY ASKED QUESTIONS

What is a fish?

Fish are aquatic, typically cold-blooded animals that have backbones, gills and fins.

Are all fish cold-blooded?

All freshwater fish are cold-blooded. Recently it has been discovered that some members of the saltwater Tuna family are warm-blooded. Whales and Bottlenose Dolphins are also warm-blooded, but they are mammals, not fish.

Do all fish have scales?

No. Most fish have scales that look like those on the Common Goldfish. A few, such as the Alligator Gar, have scales that resemble armor plates. Catfish have no scales at all.

How do fish breathe?

A fish takes in water through its mouth and forces it through its gills, where a system of fine membranes absorbs oxygen from the water and releases carbon dioxide. Gills cannot pump air efficiently over these membranes, which quickly dry out and stick together. Fish should never be out of the water longer than you can hold your breath.

Can fish breathe air?

Some species can; gar have a modified swim bladder that acts like a lung. Fish that can't breathe air may die when dissolved oxygen in the water falls below critical levels.

How do fish swim?

Fish swim by contracting bands of muscles on alternate sides of their body so the tail is whipped rapidly from side to side. Pectoral and pelvic fins are used mainly for stability when a fish hovers, but are sometimes used during rapid bursts of forward motion.

Do all fish look like fish?

Most do and are easily recognizable as fish. Eels and lampreys are fish, but they look like snakes. The Bullseye Snakehead looks like something out of a scary movie.

Where can you find fish?

Some fish species can be found in almost any body of water, but not all fish are found everywhere. Each is designed to exploit a particular habitat. A species may move around within its home water, sometimes migrating hundreds of miles between lakes, rivers and tributary streams. Some movements, such as spawning migrations, are seasonal and very predictable.

Fish may also move horizontally from one area to another or vertically in the water column in response to changes in environmental conditions and food availability. In addition, many fish have daily travel patterns. By studying a species' habitat, food and spawning information in this book—and understanding how it interacts with other Florida fish—it is possible to make an educated prediction of where to find it in any lake, stream or river.

FISH DISEASES

Fish are susceptible to various parasites, infections and diseases. Some have little effect on fish populations, while others, such as the VHS virus now invading the Great Lakes, may have devastating effects. Fish diseases are not transmitted to humans but may render the fish inedible. Care should be taken to avoid transferring a disease from one body of water to another. Information on freshwater fish diseases in Florida can be found on the Florida Fish and Wildlife Conservation Commission's website at www.myfwc.com

INVASIVE SPECIES

While introduced species can have great recreational value, as is the case of the Striped Bass hybrids, many exotic species have caused problems. Never move fish, water or vegetation from one lake or stream to another, and always follow state laws. Details are available at the Florida Fish and Wildlife Conservation Commission website: www.myfwc.com

FUN WITH FISH

There are many ways to enjoy Florida's fish, from reading about them in this book to watching them in the wild. Hands-on activities are also popular. Many resident and nonresident anglers enjoy pursuing game fish. The sport offers a great chance to enjoy the outdoors with friends and family, and in many cases, bring home a healthy meal of fresh fish.

Proceeds from license sales, along with special taxes anglers pay on fishing supplies and motorboat fuel, fund the majority of fish management efforts, including fish surveys, the development of special regulations and stocking programs. The sport also has a huge impact on Florida's economy, supporting thousands of jobs in fishing, tourism and related industries.

CATCH-AND-RELEASE FISHING

Selective harvest (keeping some fish to eat and releasing the rest) and total catch-and-release fishing allow anglers to enjoy the sport without harming the resource. Catch-and-release is especially important with certain species and sizes of fish, and in lakes or rivers where biologists are trying to improve the fishery by protecting large predators, fish of breeding age, or adult fish. The fishing regulations posted on Florida's Fish and Wildlife Conservation Commission website and your local fisheries' office are excellent sources of advice on which fish to keep and which to release.

Catch-and-release is only truly successful if the fish survives the experience. Following are helpful tips to help reduce the chances of post-release mortality.

- Play and land fish quickly.

- Wet your hands before touching a fish to avoid removing its protective slime coating.

- Handle the fish gently and keep it in the water if possible.

- Do not hold the fish by the eye sockets or gills. Hold it horizontally and support its belly.

- If a fish is deeply hooked, cut the line so at least an inch hangs outside the mouth. This helps the hook lie flush when the fish takes in food.

- Circle hooks may help reduce deeply hooked fish.

- Don't fish in deep water unless you plan to keep your catch.

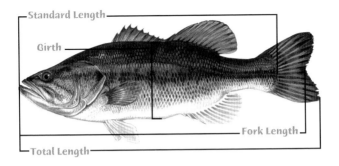

FISH MEASUREMENT

Fish are measured in three ways: standard length, fork length and total length. The first two are more accurate, because tails are often damaged or worn down. Total length is used in slot limits.

The following formulas estimate the weight of popular game fish. Lengths are in inches; weight is in pounds.

Formulas

Bass weight = (length x length x girth) / 1,200
Pike weight = (length x length x length) / 3,500
Sunfish weight = (length x length x length) / 1,200
Trout weight = (length x girth x girth) / 800
Walleye weight = (length x length x length) / 2,700

For example, let's say that you catch a 16-inch Walleye. Using the formula for Walleyes above: (16 x 16 x 16) divided by 2,700 = 1.5 pounds. Your Walleye would weigh approximately 1.5 pounds.

FLORIDA STATE RECORD FISH

SPECIES	WEIGHT (LBS.)	WHERE CAUGHT	YEAR
Bass, Butterfly Peacock	9.1	Kendall Lakes	1993
Bass, Largemouth	23.2	Big Fish Lake	1923
Bass, Redeye	7.13	Apalachicola River	1989
Bass, Spotted	3.12	Apalachicola River	1985
Bass, Striped	42.3	Apalachicola River	1993
Bass, Suwannee	3.14	Suwannee River	1985
Bass, Sunshine	16.4	Lake Seminole	1985
Bass, White	4.11	Apalachicola River	1982
Bluegill	2.15	Crystal Lake	1989
Bowfin	19.0	Lake Kissimmee	1984
Bullhead, Brown	5.12	Cedar Creek	1995
Bullhead, Yellow	2.12	Little Withlacoochee River	1955
Catfish, Blue	61.8	Little Escambia Creek	1996
Catfish, Channel	44.8	Lake Bluff	1985
Catfish, Flathead	49.6	Apalachicola River	2004
Catfish, White	18.14	Withlacoochee River	1991
Crappie, Black	3.13	Lake Talquin	1992
Flier	1.4	Lake Iamonia	1992
Gar, Alligator	123.0	Lake Panasoffkee	1985
Gar, Florida	9.7	Lake Lawne	2001
Gar, Longnose	41.0	Kankakee River	2002
Oscar	2.5	Lake Okeechobee	1994
Pickerel, Chain	6.15	Lake Talquin	1971
Pickerel, Redfin	1.1	New River	2004
Shad, American	5.3	St Johns River	1990
Sunfish, Redbreast	2.1	Suwannee River	1988
Sunfish, Redear	4.14	Merritts Mill Pond	1986
Sunfish, Spotted	0.4	Suwannee River	1984
Warmouth	2.7	Yellow River	1985

FISH CONSUMPTION ADVISORIES

Most fish are safe to eat, but pollutants in the food chain are a valid concern. The Florida Department of Health, in cooperation with the Florida Fish and Wildlife Conservation Commission, routinely monitors contaminant levels in fish and wildlife and issues advisories on contaminant levels in sport fish and wildlife taken in Florida. Advisory information can be found on the Florida DOH website, www.doh.state.fl.us or by calling (850) 245-4299.

These pages explain how the information is presented for each fish.

SAMPLE FISH ILLUSTRATION

Description: brief summary of physical characteristics to help you identify the fish, such as coloration and markings, body shape, fin size and placement

Similar Species: lists other fish that look similar and the pages on which they can be found; also includes detailed inset drawings (below) highlighting physical traits such as markings, mouth size or shape and fin characteristics to help you distinguish this fish from similar species

Largemouth Bass	Shoal Bass	Spotted Bass	Suwannee Bass
mouth extends past eye	mouth doesn't extend past eye	mouth doesn't extend past eye	mouth doesn't extend past eye

SAMPLE COMPARE ILLUSTRATIONS

22

COMMON NAME
Scientific Name

Other Names: common terms or nicknames you may hear to describe this species

Habitat: environment where the fish is found (such as streams, rivers, small or large lakes, fast-flowing or still water, in or around vegetation, near shore, in clear water)

Range: geographic distribution, starting with the fish's over-all range, followed by state-specific information

Food: what the fish eats most of the time (such as crusta-ceans, insects, fish, plankton)

Reproduction: timing of and behavior during the spawning period (dates and water temperatures, migration informa-tion, preferred spawning habitat, type of nest if applicable, colonial or solitary nester, parental care for eggs or fry)

Average Size: average length or range of length, average weight or range of weight

Records: state—the state record for this species, location and year; North American—the North American record for this species, location and year (based on the Fresh Water Fishing Hall of Fame)

Notes: Interesting natural history information. This can include unique behaviors, remarkable features, sporting and table quality, details on migrations, seasonal patterns or population trends.

Description: gray to gray-brown body with minute white spots on sides near tail; the body is long and wide at the head but narrow at the tail; head is broad and flat with 8 barbels around the mouth; small eyes; long dorsal and anal fin; rounded tail fin

Similar Species: Bullheads (pg. 30-34)

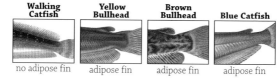

Walking Catfish	Yellow Bullhead	Brown Bullhead	Blue Catfish
no adipose fin	adipose fin	adipose fin	adipose fin

WALKING CATFISH

Clarias batrachus

Other Names: clarias catfish, snake cat

Habitat: small, shallow streams and pools with dense vegetation; very abundant in the Everglades

Range: native to Sri Lanka through eastern India to the Malay Archipelago, established in Florida, collected in Massachusetts, Georgia, Nevada, and California; widespread and locally abundant in central and southern Florida

Food: aquatic invertebrates, small crustaceans, small fish and detritus

Reproduction: adults construct nest out of submerged vegetation to hold adhesive eggs; males guard eggs and young

Average Size: 6 to 10 inches, 8 ounces to 1 pound

Records: State—none; North American—2 pounds, 10 ounces, Delray Beach, Florida, 2001

Notes: Walking Catfish have a modified gill structure that allows them to breathe air and live out of water if kept moist. They "walk" through wet terrain, often after a rain, using their pectoral fins to help them slither along. After escaping from aquaculture operations in the late '60s, they quickly spread to 20 counties in 10 years. Walking Catfish can be very abundant locally; in some areas, there are reportedly 3,000 pounds of the fish per acre. Their numbers have stabilized or are decreasing since the '90s.

Description: dark brown to black body with two rows of plate-like armor on each side; two pairs of long chin barbels; terminal mouth; breeding males have bright red pectoral fins with sharp spines

Similar Species: none

BROWN HOPLO
Hoplosternum littorale

Other Names: armored catfish, currito, cascadu, atipa, tamuata

Habitat: young fish inhabit shallow, sluggish streams, lakes, and brackish pools with dense vegetation and a soft bottom; adults prefer deeper, more open water

Range: Trinidad and eastern South America, established in Texas and Florida; central Florida from the St. Johns and Kissimmee River drainages to Lake Trafford, expanding in the north

Food: small crustaceans, aquatic insects and some plant material

Reproduction: males make a bubble nest covered with vegetation; after fertilization, eggs are moved into the nest by mouth; males guard nest and young

Average Size: 6 to 10 inches, 8 ounces to 1.5 pounds

Records: none

Notes: Brown Hoplos are small, prehistoric-looking fish introduced to Florida from South America. Hoplos have poorly developed gills and gulp air to aid in breathing. Brown Hoplos can withstand water with low oxygen levels and high hydrogen sulfide content, enabling them to inhabit sluggish backwaters where few other fish can survive. Hoplos are a highly regarded for food in their native range and are now a favorite target for cast netting in the upper St. Johns River.

Description: brownish-green back and sides with white belly;
long, stout body; rounded tail; continuous dorsal fin; bony
plates covering head; males have a large "eye" spot at the
base of the tail

Similar Species: Northern Snakehead (pg. 118), Walking
Catfish (pg. 24)

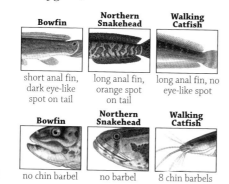

Bowfin	**Northern Snakehead**	**Walking Catfish**
short anal fin, dark eye-like spot on tail	long anal fin, orange spot on tail	long anal fin, no eye-like spot
Bowfin	**Northern Snakehead**	**Walking Catfish**
no chin barbel	no barbel	8 chin barbels

BOWFIN

Amiidae

Amia calva

Other Names: dogfish, grindle, mudfish, cypress trout, lake lawyer, beaverfish

Habitat: deep waters associated with vegetation in warm water lakes and rivers; feeds in shallow weedbeds

Range: Mississippi River drainage east through the St. Lawrence drainage, south from Texas to Florida; common throughout Florida

Food: fish, crayfish

Reproduction: in spring, when water exceeds 61 degrees, male removes vegetation to build a 2-foot nest in sand or gravel; one or more females deposit up to 5,000 eggs in nest; male tenaciously guards the nest and "ball" of young

Average Size: 12 to 24 inches, 2 to 5 pounds

Records: State—19 pounds, Lake Kissimmee, Osceola County; North American—21 pounds, 8 ounces, Forest Lake, South Carolina, 1980

Notes: A voracious predator, the Bowfin prowls shallow weedbeds preying on anything that moves. Once thought detrimental to game fish populations, it is now considered an asset in controlling rough fish and stunted game fish. An air breather that tolerates low oxygen levels, the Bowfin can survive buried in mud for short periods during droughts. It is not commonly fished for but is often caught by bass fishermen. Mostly thought of as a nuisance, Bowfins outfight most game fish. The flesh is jelly-like and not highly regarded by most anglers, but tasty when prepared correctly. **29**

Description: yellowish-brown upper body; mottled back and sides; barbels around mouth; adipose fin; scaleless skin; rounded tail; well-defined barbs on the pectoral spines

Similar Species: Tadpole Madtom (pg. 42), White Catfish (pg. 40), Yellow Bullhead (pg. 32)

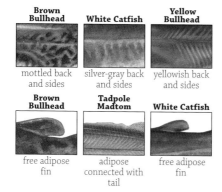

Brown Bullhead	White Catfish	Yellow Bullhead
mottled back and sides	silver-gray back and sides	yellowish back and sides

Brown Bullhead	Tadpole Madtom	White Catfish
free adipose fin	adipose connected with tail	free adipose fin

BROWN BULLHEAD

Ameiurus nebulosus

Other Names: marbled or speckled bullhead, red cat

Habitat: warm, weedy lakes and sluggish streams

Range: southern Canada through the Great Lakes down the eastern states to Florida, introduced in the West; common throughout Florida except in the far south

Food: insects, fish, fish eggs, snails, some plant matter

Reproduction: in early summer, males build a nest in shallow water amid vegetation and above a sandy or rocky bottom; both sexes guard the eggs and young

Average Size: 8 to 10 inches, 4 ounces to 2 pounds

Records: State—5 pounds, 11.5 ounces, Cedar Creek, Duval County, 1995; North American—6 pounds, 2 ounces, Pearl River, Mississippi, 1991

Notes: The Brown Bullhead is the most abundant catfish in Florida and can be found in turbid backwaters as well as in clear lakes and streams. The adults are very involved in rearing their young, first by agitating the eggs, then by guarding the fry until they are about an inch long. Like other catfish, bullheads are nocturnal feeders. Brown Bullheads are not strong fighters, but are easily caught fishing on the bottom with worms or dough balls made from corn flakes and bread. The Brown Bullhead's reddish meat is tasty and fine table fare when taken from clear water.

31

Description: olive head and back; yellowish-green head and sides; white belly; barbels on lower jaw are pale green or white; adipose fin; scaleless skin; rounded tail

Similar Species: Brown Bullhead (pg. 30), Tadpole Madtom (pg. 42), White Catfish (pg. 40)

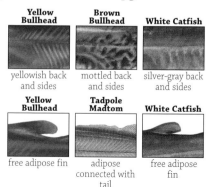

Yellow Bullhead	Brown Bullhead	White Catfish
yellowish back and sides	mottled back and sides	silver-gray back and sides

Yellow Bullhead	Tadpole Madtom	White Catfish
free adipose fin	adipose connected with tail	free adipose fin

YELLOW BULLHEAD

Ameiurus natalis

Other Names: white-whiskered bullhead, yellow cat

Habitat: warm, weedy lakes and sluggish streams

Range: southern Great Lakes through the eastern half of the U.S. to the Gulf and into Mexico, introduced in the West; common throughout Florida

Food: insects, crayfish, snails, small fish, some plant matter

Reproduction: in late spring to early summer, males build a nest in shallow water with some vegetation and a soft bottom; both sexes guard the eggs and young

Average Size: 8 to 10 inches, 1 to 2 pounds

Records: State—2 pounds, 12 ounces, Little Withlacoochee River, Sumter County, 2003; North American—4 pounds, 15 ounces, Ogeechee River, Georgia, 2003

Notes: The Yellow Bullhead is the bullhead species least tolerant of turbidity and it is more commonly found in clear streams or ponds than other bullheads. Bullheads feed by "taste," locating food by following chemical trails through the water. This ability can be greatly diminished in polluted water, impairing the bullhead's ability to find food. The Yellow Bullhead is less likely than other bullheads to overpopulate a lake and become stunted. Yellow Bullheads are easily caught with worms or cut bait throughout the day but are more active at night. The creamy, white flesh is firm and tasty when the fish are taken from clean water.

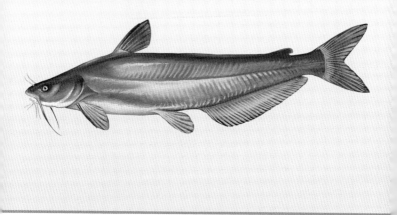

Description: body pale blue to slate gray; hump in back at dorsal fin; long anal fin with straight rear edge; forked tail, adipose fin; no scales; chin barbels

Similar Species: Channel Catfish (pg. 36), White Catfish (pg. 40)

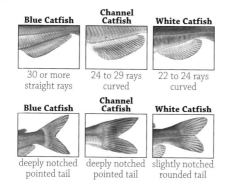

Blue Catfish	Channel Catfish	White Catfish
30 or more straight rays	24 to 29 rays curved	22 to 24 rays curved
deeply notched pointed tail	deeply notched pointed tail	slightly notched rounded tail

BLUE CATFISH

Ictalurus furcatus

Ictaluridae

Other Names: humpback, river, forktail, great blue, chuckle-head, silver or Missouri cat, blue fulton

Habitat: deep pools of large rivers with hard bottoms and moderate to strong currents; a few reservoirs

Range: the Mississippi River watershed and into Mexico, stocked in some Atlantic coast streams; large rivers in the Florida Panhandle south to the Suwannee River

Food: fish, crayfish

Reproduction: spawns when water reaches the low 80s; males build and defend nest in undercut banks or other sheltered areas; males guard young for a short period

Average Size: 20 to 30 inches, 15 to 25 pounds

Records: State—61 pounds, 8 ounces, Little Escambia Creek, Escambia County, 1996; North American—124 pounds, Mississippi River, Illinois, 2005

Notes: The Blue Catfish is the largest North American catfish. They prefer fast currents in large rivers, often congregating in the fast water below power generating dams and feeding on fish that pass through the turbines. Large Channel Catfish are often mistaken for Blue Catfish, and this has led to a great deal of confusion. In fact, Florida's first Blue Catfish catch was not officially recorded until 1990. Blue Catfish could be detrimental if transported, as they could become established in other Florida streams and have the potential to reduce native game fish populations.

Description: steel gray to silver on the back and sides; white belly; black spots on the sides; large fish lack spots and appear dark olive or slate gray; forked tail; adipose fin; long barbels around mouth

Similar Species: Bullheads (pp. 30-32), White Catfish (pg. 40)

Channel Catfish / **Bullheads**

deeply forked tail

tail rounded or slightly notched

Channel Catfish

24-30 rays in anal fin, spots

White Catfish

22 to 24 rays in anal fin, no spots

Channel Catfish / **White Catfish**

spots on young fish

sides lack spots

CHANNEL CATFISH

Ictalurus punctatus

Other Names: spotted, speckled or silver catfish, fiddler

Habitat: medium to large streams with deep pools, low to moderate current and sand, gravel or rubble bottom; also found in warm lakes; tolerates turbid (cloudy) conditions

Range: southern Canada through the Midwest into Mexico and Florida, widely introduced; common throughout Florida except the Keys

Food: insects, crustaceans, fish, some plant matter

Reproduction: matures at 2 to 4 years; in summer, when water temperature reaches about 70 to 85 degrees, male builds a nest in a dark, sheltered area such as an undercut bank; female deposits 2,000 to 21,000 eggs, which hatch in 6 to 10 days; male guards eggs and young until the nest is deserted

Average Size: 12 to 20 inches, 3 to 4 pounds

Records: State—44 pounds, 8 ounces, Lake Bluff, Lake County, 1985; North American—58 pounds, Santee Cooper Reservoir, South Carolina, 1964

Notes: Channel Catfish are one of the most sought after fish in the Southern U.S. They can put up a strong fight and are fine table fare. Like other catfish, Channels are nocturnal and are most successfully fished for at night. Channel Catfish were the first widely farmed fish in the U.S. and are now common in grocery stores and restaurants throughout the country. Though not considered a game fish in Florida, they are harvested for the commercial market as well as for sport.

Description: color variable, body and head usually mottled yellow or brown; belly cream to yellow; head broad and flattened; pronounced underbite; adipose fin; chin barbels

Similar Species: Blue Catfish (pg. 34), Channel Catfish (pg. 36)

Flathead Catfish	**Blue Catfish**	**Channel Catfish**
rounded tail	deeply notched, pointed tail	deeply notched, pointed tail

Flathead Catfish	**Blue Catfish**	**Channel Catfish**
14 to 17 small rays in anal fin	30 or more straight rays in anal fin	24 to 30 curved rays in anal fin,

FLATHEAD CATFISH

Pylodictis olivaris

Other Names: shovelnose, shovelhead, yellow, mud, pied, johnnie or Mississippi cat, goujon, opelousas

Habitat: deep pools of large rivers and impoundments

Range: the Mississippi River watershed and into Mexico; large rivers in the Southwest, stocked in the Southeast; Apalachicola and Escambia Rivers in Florida's Panhandle and a few other scattered lakes in northern Florida

Food: fish, crayfish

Reproduction: spawns when water is 72 to 80 degrees; male builds and defends nest in hollow logs, undercut banks or other sheltered areas; large females may lay up to 30,000 eggs

Average Size: 20 to 30 inches, 10 to 20 pounds

Records: State—49 pounds, 6 ounces, Apalachicola River, Gulf County, 2004; North American—123 pounds, Elk River Reservoir, Kansas, 1998

Notes: A large, solitary predator that feeds aggressively on live fish at night. Often, Flatheads enter shallow water seeking prey on the surface, but they are found more frequently near logjams or in deep pools. Flatheads have been introduced into some lakes in an attempt to control stunted panfish populations. Some of these introductions have led to reductions in popular game fish populations. A strong, tenacious fighter with firm, white flesh, Flatheads are highly prized by many anglers.

39

Description: bluish-silver body and off-white belly; older fish dark blue with some mottling; forked tail with pointed lobes; lacks scales; adipose fin; white chin barbels

Similar Species: Channel Catfish (pg. 36)

White Catfish	**Channel Catfish**	**White Catfish**	**Channel Catfish**
22 to 24 rays in anal fin, no spots	24 to 30 rays in anal fin	spots on young fish	spots on sides

WHITE CATFISH

Ameiurus catus

Other Names: silver or weed catfish, whitey

Habitat: fresh to slightly brackish water of coastal streams; shallow lakes with good vegetation and a firm bottom

Range: Maine south to Florida and west to Texas, introduced in some Western states; common statewide in Florida's fresh and brackish waters

Food: insects, crayfish, small fish, some plant debris

Reproduction: male builds nest in sheltered areas with a sand or gravel bottom when water temperatures reach the high 60s; both sexes guard nest and eggs until fry disperse

Average Size: 10 to 18 inches, 1 to 2 pounds

Records: State—18 pounds, 14 ounces, Withlacoochee River, Marion County, 1991; North American—22 pounds, William Land Park Pond, California, 1994

Notes: The White Catfish is an abundant species in Florida's fresh water, as well as in the brackish coastal waters. In terms of habits, White Catfish are intermediate between Channel Catfish and Bullheads. White Catfish prefer quieter water than Channel Catfish and prefer a somewhat firmer bottom than that sought by bullheads. They frequent the edge of reedbeds and are often caught when still-fishing the bottom near deep water. They are somewhat less nocturnal than other catfish. While they are not thought of as a great sport fish, they are quite popular with Florida's catfish fishermen and have firm flesh and fine flavor.

TADPOLE MADTOM

MARGINED MADTOM

Description: Tadpole—dark olive to brown; dark line on side; jaws even; Margined—gray to tan; protruding upper jaw; fin margins black; both—large, fleshy head with barbels at mouth; adipose fin connected to tail fin

Similar Species: Bullheads (pp. 30-32), Catfish (pp. 34-40)

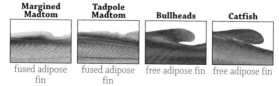

Margined Madtom	Tadpole Madtom	Bullheads	Catfish
fused adipose fin	fused adipose fin	free adipose fin	free adipose fin

TADPOLE MADTOM

Noturus gyrinus

MARGINED MADTOM *Noturus insignis*

Other Names: willow or tadpole cat, tadpole stonecat, river or creek madtom

Habitat: Tadpole—vegetated water near shore in medium to large lakes; Margined—rocky stream and creek riffles

Range: eastern U.S. from the Gulf through the Great Lake states; common throughout Florida

Food: small invertebrates, algae and other plant matter

Reproduction: both spawn in late spring; females lay eggs under objects such as roots, rocks, logs or in abandoned crayfish burrows; nest guarded by adults

Average Size: 3 to 4 inches

Records: none

Notes: The Tadpole Madtom is the most widespread madtom of the three species that inhabit Florida. All three are small, secretive fish that are most active at night. Madtoms have poison glands under their skin at the base of the dorsal and pectoral fins. Though not lethal, the poison produces a painful burning sensation. Madtoms are hardy little fish and a popular baitfish in some areas. Reportedly, damaging the "slime" coating (by rolling them in sand) to make handling easier reduces their effectiveness as bait.

Description: yellow-green to red-brown body and fins; large
  black blotch on sides; smaller blotches on gill and tail; long
  slender body with round tail fin; large adults have a dark
  green body with turquoise spots; bright red from chin to the
  anal fin and far up both sides; red pectoral and dorsal fin

Similar Species: none

Cichlidae

AFRICAN JEWELFISH

Hemichromis bimaculatus

Other Names: African jewel fish, jewel molly

Habitat: shallow, weedy water in streams, canals and swamps with a soft bottom

Range: northern Africa; south Florida, Everglades and Big Cypress National Parks

Food: algae and leafy aquatic plants, small fish

Reproduction: adhesive eggs are released in heavy vegetation over an extended season; both parents guard eggs and young

Average Size: 3 to 4 inches

Records: none

Notes: When young, African Jewelfish are rather dull, small fish, but when they reach full adult breeding colors they are striking. This popular aquarium fish and 30-plus other exotic species are now well established in Florida's waters. Restricted to southern Florida, Jewelfish can often be spotted at the edges of pools and canals in Dade County and the Everglades.

Description: dark green to yellow body; 6 to 7 olive to dark brown bars on sides; pectoral fins yellow, other fins blue-gray; narrow dark stripe from gill to mid-body; two dark blotches, one about mid-fish, one at the base of the tail; body spot fades in older fish; long feathery tips to anal and dorsal fins

Similar Species: Mayan Cichlid (pg. 52)

Black Acara	Mayan Cichlid
two spots on sides, vertical stripe	large spot on tail but not on sides, no vertical stripe

BLACK ACARA
Cichlasoma bimaculatum

Other Names: two-spot or port cichlid

Habitat: shallow, weedy water in streams, canals and swamps

Range: native in Guyana and Venezuela; southern Florida, Lake Okeechobee and possibly the Tampa area

Food: algae and leafy aquatic plants, small fish

Reproduction: adhesive eggs are released in heavy vegetation over an extended season; both parents guard eggs and young

Average Size: 3 to 6 inches, 4 ounces

Records: none

Notes: In the early '60s Black Acaras raised for the pet industry escaped and became established in Hillsborough and Manatee Counties. By the late '70s they were no longer present in these counties but were well established in southern Florida. Black Acara can withstand low oxygen levels and often become the dominant fish in shallow, swampy areas. Feisty, but too small to be an important panfish, Acaras could have a negative impact on native fish populations.

BUTTERFLY PEACOCK BASS

SPECKLED PEACOCK BASS

Description: (Butterfly) dark green to black back; yellow to creamy sides with three dark yellow tinged blotches; lower fins red to pink; large dark spot with light margin on upper lob of tail; red eye; bass shaped body with large terminal mouth

Similar Species: Speckled Peacock Bass

Butterfly Peacock Bass	Speckled Peacock Bass	Butterfly Peacock Bass	Speckled Peacock Bass
dark blotches on sides, hump on back	3 dark bars on side, no hump on back	small dark specks on gills	large dark blotch on gills

BUTTERFLY PEACOCK BASS
Cichla ocellaris

SPECKLED PEACOCK BASS *Cichla temensis*

Other Names: peacock bass, peacock pavon, butterfly bass, butterfly cichlid

Habitat: lakes, rivers, and coastal canals with good shade and temperatures in excess of 60 degrees throughout the year

Range: the Amazon basin in South America and introduced in Puerto Rico, Hawaii, Texas and Florida; Miami-Dade and Broward Counties in Florida

Food: small fish

Reproduction: spawns throughout the summer months; a cleared flat, hard surface along the shoreline is selected for a nest; adults guard eggs and young

Average Size: 12 to 18 inches, 2 to 5 pounds

Records: State—9 pounds, 1 ounce, Kendall Lakes, Dade County, 1993; North American—9 pounds, 1 ounce, Kendall Lakes, Florida, 1993

Notes: In the early '80s, Peacock Bass were introduced into Florida as a sport fish and to control abundant exotic forage fish. Today, Butterfly Peacock Bass are one of the most popular sport fish in southeastern Florida. Butterfly Peacocks are locally very abundant in some Dade County canals. Speckled Peacock bass are larger fish and much less common. In fact, they are protected and should be released. Though it is legal to keep Butterfly Peacocks, they too should be released, as they aid in the control of the smaller exotic cichlids that now crowd many Florida canals.

49

Description: dark green back; dusky yellow sides with purple sheen and row of black squares; body covered with many small dark blotches; large, oblique, toothed mouth with protruding lower lip; red eye; dorsal and anal fins pointed

Similar Species: Black Crappie (pg. 144)

Jaguar Guapote

large toothed mouth

Black Crappie

smaller mouth, no teeth

JAGUAR GUAPOTE

Cichlasoma managuense

Other Names: tiger fish, Managuense cichlid, guapote tiger

Habitat: lakes, slow-moving streams and canals with thick vegetation

Range: Atlantic slope of Central and South America, introduced to Mexico and U.S.; coastal canals of southeastern Florida

Food: small fish, insects and crayfish

Reproduction: spawns from spring through fall; adhesive eggs laid on a hard, flat surface near weedbeds; adults guard eggs and young

Average Size: 8 to 12 inches, 1 pound to 1 pound, 8 ounces

Records: State—none; North American—3 pounds, 11 ounces, Kendall Lakes, Florida, 2006, (IGFA) not recorded as state record

Notes: Jaguar Guapote are aggressive predators that eat just about anything they can swallow. They were introduced into Mexico as a food and sport fish, with devastating consequences for native fish populations. The Florida population probably originated from escaped aquarium fish as Jaguar Guapote are popular pets. They are a very popular sport fish in Mexico, readily taking artificial lures and giving a long, hard fight. Guapotes are highly regarded as food in Central America.

Description: olive-brown body with 5 to 7 green-black vertical bars; silver-blue spot with black center on upper lobe of tail; pink chin and breast that is brighter during breeding season; broken lateral line; rounder dorsal, anal and tail fin

Similar Species: Oscar (pg. 56), Spotted Tilapia (pg. 60)

Mayan Cichlid	**Oscar**	**Spotted Tilapia**
silver-green tail spot, pointed dorsal and anal fin	orange-red spot on tail, rounded dorsal and anal fins	no tail spot, pointed tail and anal fins

MAYAN CICHLID

Cichlasoma urophthalmus

Other Names: orange tiger

Habitat: weedy coastal streams and lakes; brackish lagoons; highly adaptable

Range: western slope of Central America; abundant in Florida south of Lake Okeechobee including Florida Bay in the Everglades

Food: aquatic invertebrates and small fish

Reproduction: colonial spawners in early spring; adults build a small, round nest or use a cleared, hard surface; eggs and young are both guarded

Average Size: 6 to 10 inches, 8 ounces to 1 pound

Records: State—none; North American—2 pounds, 8 ounces, Holiday Park, Florida, 1999, (IGFA, not recorded as state record)

Notes: Mayan Cichlids are small, but very aggressive, hard-fighting panfish that are expanding their range in southern Florida. They readily take both live and artificial bait and are becoming a favorite panfish, particularly for fly fishermen. Mayan Cichlids prefer brackish water, but are very adaptable and are now common in most waters south of Lake Okeechobee.

Description: dark phase—gray body with dark bars or spots on side; light phase—orange, red or white with very faint dark bars; light phase may have dark or orange blotches on back; all young are gray; breeding males have hump on forehead

Similar Species: Spotted Tilapia (pg. 60)

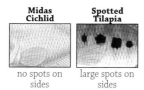

Midas Cichlid	Spotted Tilapia
no spots on sides	large spots on sides

MIDAS CICHLID

Cichlasoma citrinellum

Other Names: orange tiger, gold or humped bream, red devil

Habitat: coastal canals and streams with rock overhangs or crevices for cover; a few lakes

Range: Atlantic slope of Nicaragua and Costa Rica, introduced into Hawaii, Puerto Rico and Florida; common in the Black Creek and Cutler Drain canal system in Miami-Dade County

Food: aquatic invertebrates, snails and small fish

Reproduction: adhesive eggs are attached to substrate; both parents guard eggs and young; young feed on mucus that is secreted from the parents' sides

Average Size: 6 to 10 inches, 12 ounces to 1 pound, 8 ounces

Records: State—none; North American—2 pounds, 8 ounces, Miami Canal, Florida, 2004 (IGFA, not recorded as a state record)

Notes: Midas Cichlids have two color phases. The dark phase is the most common in Central America, whereas the light phase is common in Florida. About 10% of the adult Midas cichlids are dark in Florida; all of the young are gray. Bright Midas Cichlids are very popular aquarium fish around the world and are the source of Florida's wild population. Unlike other cichlids, this fish is not aggressive and is hard to entice with a baited hook, but Midas Cichlids are good table fare if you can catch them.

Description: dark brown to black body with rust to orange mottling; orange to red spot with black center on upper lobe of tail; round, thick body; dorsal tail and anal fin rounded and fan like; very slimy

Similar Species: Warmouth (pg. 160)

Oscar	Warmouth
orange-red spot on base of tail, rounded dorsal and anal fin	no tail spot, pointed tail and anal fin

56

OSCAR

Astronotus ocellatus

Other Names: spot perch, spot bream

Habitat: lakes, canals and swampy pools with good vegetation

Range: the Orinoco, La Plata and Amazon River basins in South America; in Florida, from Lake Okeechobee south

Food: small fish, insects and crayfish

Reproduction: spawns throughout the summer months on cleared, flat areas along the shoreline; adults guard eggs and young

Average Size: 8 to 10 inches, 8 ounces to 12 ounces

Records: State—2 pounds, 5 ounces, Lake Okeechobee, Palm Beach County, 1994; North American—3 pounds, 8 ounces, Pasadena Lakes, 1999

Notes: Oscars are popular aquarium fish that have escaped and are now established in southern Florida. Oscars are now the most sought after panfish from Lake Okeechobee south. This warmwater fish requires temperatures over 60 degrees year-round and sometimes suffers from winter die-offs north of the Everglades. They are aggressive feeders, and readily take both artificial and natural bait.

Description: blue-gray head and body with faint dark bars; pink to red borders on dorsal and caudal fins; white belly; young have a dark spot on rear of dorsal fin; continuous soft and hard rayed dorsal fin;

Similar Species: It is hard to differentiate the Blue Tilapia from the Mozambique Tilapia, as they interbreed with one another, but the Mozambique Tilapia has a limited range from Titusville south

BLUE TILAPIA
Oreochromius aureus

Other Names: Israeli tilapia, gray bream

Habitat: warm, weedy lakes and streams; brackish and coastal salt water

Range: Native to northern Africa and the Middle East, widely introduced around the world as a food fish; common throughout Florida

Food: green algae and other plankton

Reproduction: males build small round nests and lure in females; female broods eggs in her mouth; young return to mother's mouth for protection until about three weeks old

Average Size: 8 to 12 inches, 2 to 3 pounds

Records: State—none; North American—9 pounds, Kissimmee Lake, 2003 (IGFA, not recorded as state record)

Notes: Tilapia are one of the most widely-farmed food fish in the world. Several species have been collected or are established in Florida and many are now interbreeding with other species and becoming difficult to differentiate. The Blue Tilapia is the largest and most widespread species, and the one causing the most problems. Blue Tilapia compete with native species for food and living space and destroy natural habitat. Tilapia are excellent eating but do not often take baited hooks; they are now becoming a popular target for bow fishermen.

59

Description: yellow-green to bronze body; line of dark spots along sides that appear as bars in young fish; black stripe through eye; pointed dorsal and anal fin

Similar Species: Oscar (pg. 56)

Spotted Tilapia

no tail spot, pointed tail and anal fin

Oscar

spot on tail, rounded dorsal and anal fin

SPOTTED TILAPIA

Tilapia mariae

Other Names: Niger or black mangrove cichlid, greenies, African bream

Habitat: warm, weedy lakes and streams; brackish lagoons; highly adaptable

Range: Native to Africa, introduced in Florida, Arizona, Nevada and Australia; common in southern Florida, abundant in Brevard County

Food: green algae and other plankton

Reproduction: colonial spawners from November to March, adhesive eggs are laid on the undersides of hard surfaces; adults guard eggs and young; young fish attach a thin thread from the head to substrate to prevent drifting

Average Size: 6 to 10 inches, 8 ounces to 1.5 pounds

Records: State—none; North American—4 pounds, Plantation, Florida, 2005 (IGFA, not recorded as a state record)

Notes: Spotted Tilapia escaped from fish farms and were first collected in Florida in the early '70s. They soon became very abundant, making up 25% of the fish in some canals, and replacing the Black Acara as the dominant fish. Butterfly Peacock Bass were introduced to help control Spotted Tilapia. There are several species of Tilapia now established in Florida; many are hybridizing and are now hard to differentiate from other species. As algae-feeders, Spotted Tilapia do not aggressively take baited hooks, but they are good table fare when caught. **61**

Description: dark brown on top with yellow sides and white belly; long, snake-like body with large mouth; pectoral fins; gill slits; continuous dorsal, tail and anal fin

Similar Species: Bowfin (pg. 28), Southern Brook Lamprey (pg. 82), Swamp Eel (pg. 162)

American Eel	**Southern Brook Lamprey**	**Swamp Eel**
pectoral fins	mouth is a sucking disk	no pectoral fins

American Eel	**Bowfin**
continuous dorsal tail and anal fin	one dorsal fin, short anal fin

AMERICAN EEL

Anguilla rostrata

Anguillidae

Other Names: common, Boston, Atlantic or freshwater eel

Habitat: soft bottoms of medium to large streams; brackish tidewater areas

Range: the Atlantic Ocean, eastern and central North America and eastern Central America; possible in any Florida waters with coastal access

Food: insects, crayfish, small fish

Reproduction: a "catadromous" species that spends most of its life in freshwater, returning to the Sargasso Sea in the North Atlantic Ocean to spawn; females lay up to 20 million eggs; adults die after spawning

Average Size: 24 to 36 inches, 1 to 3 pounds

Records: State—none; North American—8 pounds, 8 ounces, Cliff Pond, Massachusetts, 1992

Notes: Leaf-shaped larval eels drift with ocean currents for about a year. When they reach the river mouths of North and Central America, they morph into small eels (elvers). Males remain in the estuaries; females migrate upstream. At maturity (up to 20 years of age), adults return to the Sargasso Sea. Once commercially harvested, they are now sought only by a few anglers for sport and food. Smoked eels have an excellent flavor.

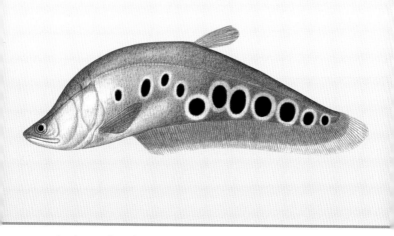

Description: silver body with black spots ringed in white; spots get larger approaching the tail; long anal fin; feather-shaped body

Similar Species: none

CLOWN KNIFEFISH

Notopterus chitala

Other Names: silver knifefish, featherback

Habitat: lakes, streams and canals with rock and vegetation for cover

Range: Southeast Asia; in Florida, Lake Osborne to the Lake Ida system in Palm Beach County

Food: aquatic insects, crustaceans and small fish

Reproduction: in spring, adhesive eggs are attached to substrate where males fan eggs, then guard the young

Average Size: 10 to 18 inches, 1 to 3 pounds

Records: none

Notes: This exotic-looking fish has long been a popular aquarium fish, and the Florida population probably originated from released pets. Knifefish are air-breathers and can withstand low oxygen levels and very warm water. Knifefish often feed by standing upright in the water. They are strong fighters and make spectacular leaps, making them an exciting catch for bass fishermen in the Miami area. Knifefish are highly regarded as food in their native range.

65

Description: olive to brown body mottled toward the head, but spotted at the rear and on rear fins; long, cylindrical profile; single dorsal fin located just above the anal fin; body encased in hard, plate-like scales; broad snout; two rows of large teeth on each side of upper jaw

Similar Species: Florida Gar (pg. 68), Longnose Gar (pg. 70), Spotted Gar (pg. 72)

Alligator Gar	**Florida Gar**	**Longnose Gar**	**Spotted Gar**
double row of large teeth on each side of upper jaw, no spots on head	distance from front of eye to back of gill less than two-thirds snout length, spots on head	snout twice the length of the rest of head, no spots on head	distance from front of eye to back of gill more than two-thirds snout length, spots on head

ALLIGATOR GAR
Atractosteus spatula

Lepisosteidae

Other Names: garfish, spotted gar

Habitat: backwaters of large rivers

Range: northeastern Mexico, north up the Mississippi basin to the Missouri and the lower Ohio Rivers; the Escambia, Yellow, and Choctawhatchee Rivers in the Florida Panhandle, and the Econfina/Bear Creek area in Bay County

Food: fish

Reproduction: adhesive eggs are deposited in weedy shallows when water temperatures reach the high 60s; no parental care

Average Size: 36 to 48 inches, 30 to 60 pounds

Records: State—123 pounds, Choctawhatchee River, Walton County, 1995; North American—279 pounds, Rio Grande River, Texas, 1951

Notes: The Alligator Gar is one of the most spectacular fish in North America, reaching 8 feet in length and nearly 300 pounds. Like other gar, their hard mouths and sharp teeth make them difficult to hook and land. Over most of their range they are now quite rare, but a reasonable population still exists in Florida. Alligator Gar prefer deep backwater pools in large rivers, but they occasionally enter brackish water and even salt water at river mouths.

Description: olive to brown with dark spots on the body and fins; large, round spots on top of head; long, cylindrical profile; single dorsal fin located just above the anal fin; body encased in hard, plate-like scales; broad snout; needle-sharp teeth on both jaws

Similar Species: Alligator Gar (pg. 66), Longnose Gar (pg. 70), Spotted Gar (pg. 72)

Florida Gar	**Alligator Gar**	**Longnose Gar**	**Spotted Gar**
distance from front of eye to back of gill less than two-thirds snout length	double row of large teeth on each side of upper jaw	snout twice the length of the rest of head	distance from front of eye to back of gill more than two-thirds snout length

FLORIDA GAR

Lepisosteus platyrhincus

Other Names: garfish, spotted gar

Habitat: quiet water of larger rivers and lakes

Range: eastern Florida, north through coastal Georgia to South Carolina; common from southeastern peninsular Florida to the Everglades

Food: minnows and other small fish

Reproduction: large, green eggs are deposited in weedy shallows when water temperatures reach the high 60s; using a small disc on the snout, newly hatched gar attach to something solid until their digestive tracts develop enough to allow feeding

Average Size: 18 to 30 inches, 4 to 6 pounds

Records: State—9 pounds, 7 ounces, Lake Lawne, Florida, 2001; North American—9 pounds, 7 ounces, Orange County, Florida, 2001

Notes: Very closely related to the Spotted Gar, The Florida Gar is found only in the eastern peninsula of Florida. Gar float near the surface in small groups, waiting to ambush prey with a quick sideways lunge. Florida Gar are particularly abundant and visible along the Tamiami Canal. They can be very prolific; 2,000 were taken from a 300-foot section of one canal. Gar are good fighters, but hard to hook. The flesh has a very strong, fishy flavor, and gar eggs are poisonous to mammals.

Description: olive to brown with dark spots along sides; long, cylindrical profile; single dorsal fin located just above the anal fin; body encased in hard, plate-like scales; snout twice as long as head; needle-sharp teeth on both jaws

Similar Species: Alligator Gar (pg. 66), Florida Gar (pg. 68), Spotted Gar (pg. 72)

Longnose Gar	**Alligator Gar**	**Florida Gar**	**Spotted Gar**
snout twice the length of the rest of head	double row of large teeth on each side of upper jaw	distance from front of eye to back of gill less than two-thirds snout length	distance from front of eye to back of gill more than two-thirds snout length

LONGNOSE GAR

Lepisosteus osseus

Lepisosteidae

Other Names: garfish

Habitat: quiet water of larger rivers and lakes

Range: central U.S. throughout the Mississippi drainage south into Mexico, a few rivers in the northeast Great Lakes drainages; in Florida, common from Lake Okeechobee north

Food: minnows and other small fish

Reproduction: large, green eggs are deposited in weedy shallows when water temperatures reach the high 60s; using a small disc on the snout, newly hatched gar attach to something solid until their digestive tracts develop enough to allow feeding

Average Size: 24 to 36 inches, 10 to 15 pounds

Records: State—41 pounds, Lake Panasoffkee, Sumter County, 1985; North American—50 pounds, 5 ounces, Trinity River, Texas, 1954

Notes: Gar belong to a prehistoric family of fish that can breathe air with the aid of a modified swim bladder. This adaptation makes them well-suited to survive in increasingly polluted, slow-moving rivers and lakes. Gar are a valuable asset in controlling growing populations of rough fish in these waters. They hunt by floating motionless, then making a quick, sideways slash to capture prey. Longnose Gar are the most numerous and widespread gar species in Florida.

Description: back and sides olive-brown to black-tan below, brown or black spots on head, body and fins; moderately long snout with only one row of teeth on upper jaw; young often have dark stripes on their sides and back

Similar Species: Alligator Gar (pg. 66), Florida Gar (pg. 68), Longnose Gar (pg. 70)

Spotted Gar	Alligator Gar	Florida Gar	Longnose Gar
distance from front of eye to back of gill more than two-thirds snout length, spots on head	double row of large teeth on each side of upper jaw, no spots on head	distance from front of eye to back of gill less than two-thirds snout length, spots on head	snout twice the length of the rest of head, no spots on head

Lepisosteidae

SPOTTED GAR
Lepisosteus oculatus

Other Names: garfish

Habitat: quiet water of larger to medium rivers and lakes with good vegetation

Range: central U.S. throughout the Mississippi drainage to the southern Great Lakes, east to western Florida, west to Texas; in Florida, in the Panhandle west from the Apalachicola drainage

Food: minnows and other small fish

Reproduction: adhesive eggs are deposited in weedy shallows when water temperatures reach the high 60s; using a small disc on the snout, newly hatched gar attach to something solid until their digestive tracts develop enough to allow feeding

Average Size: 18 to 30 inches, 4 to 6 pounds

Records: State—none; North American—28 pounds, 8 ounces, Lake Seminole, Florida, 1887

Notes: The Spotted Gar is a small gar common to the central U.S., but it is rare in Florida, where it is found only in the western Panhandle. In the rest of Florida, the similar, but larger, Florida Gar is the dominant species. The Spotted and Florida Gar sometimes frequent slightly brackish water, but both are much more common in fresh water. Spotted Gar seem to prefer denser vegetation than other gar. Small Spotted Gar are popular aquarium fish.

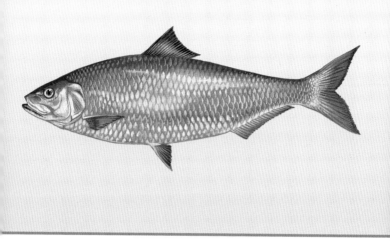

Description: silver body and blue-gray back; one dark spot on the shoulder; mouth large extending to back of eye; dark spots on lower jaw; sawtooth edge formed by sharply pointed scales along the belly (scutes); upper and lower jaw same length

Similar Species: American Shad (pg. 76), Skipjack Herring (pg. 80), Gizzard Shad (pg. 78)

Alabama Shad	American Shad	Skipjack Herring	Gizzard Shad
one dark spot on shoulder, no jaw teeth, upper and lower jaw are same length	mouth extends to back of eye, jaws even	lower jaw protruding over snout, no dark spot on shoulder, teeth on lower jaw	snout protruding over mouth, one dark spot on shoulder

ALABAMA SHAD

Alosa alabamae

Other Names: river herring, silver or 'bama shad

Habitat: coastal marine areas for most of the year; migrates up large rivers to spawn

Range: northern Gulf from Florida to Mississippi north through the Mississippi basin to the lower Ohio drainage; large rivers in the Florida Panhandle

Food: marine plankton feeders

Reproduction: migrates up spawning rivers when water temperatures reach 62 to 67 degrees; spawning takes place at night when eggs are released in moderate currents over sand or gravel

Average Size: 10 to 18 inches, 8 ounces to 1.5 pounds

Records: none

Notes: The Alabama Shad are marine fish that enter large rivers to spawn, sometimes traveling hundreds of miles upstream. Once abundant enough to be commercially harvested, increased river turbidity and dam construction have greatly reduced the Alabama Shad population over most of its range. The only large remaining population spawns in the Apalachicola River in the Florida Panhandle.

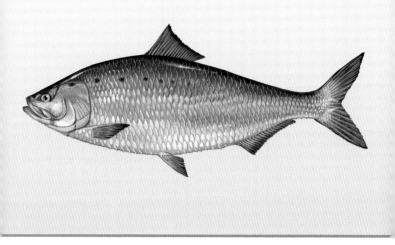

Description: silver body and blue-gray back; three or more dark spots on the shoulder; body deep and laterally compressed; large mouth extending to back of eye; sawtooth edge of sharply pointed scales along the belly (scutes)

Similar Species: Alabama Shad (pg. 74), Gizzard Shad (pg. 78), Skipjack Herring (pg. 80)

American Shad	Alabama Shad	Skipjack Herring	Gizzard Shad
mouth extends to back of eye, jaws even	one dark spot on shoulder, no jaw teeth, upper and lower jaw same length	lower jaw protruding over snout, no dark spot on shoulder, teeth on lower jaw	snout protruding over mouth, one dark spot on shoulder

AMERICAN SHAD

Alosa sapidissima

Other Names: river, silver or white shad

Habitat: coastal marine most of the year; migrates up large rivers to spawn; landlocked in a few areas

Range: Atlantic coast and associated spawning rivers from Newfoundland to Florida, introduced and established on the Pacific coast; coastal rivers in northeast Florida, primarily the St. Johns and Nassau Rivers

Food: plankton, crustaceans, small fish

Reproduction: American Shad migrate up spawning rivers when water temperatures reach 62 to 67 degrees; spawning takes place at night in the large rivers at the mouth of tributary streams; in the north, adults return to the sea after spawning; in southern states, they often die after spawning

Average Size: 18 to 20 inches, 2 to 3 pounds

Records: State—5 pounds, 3 ounces, St Johns River, Seminole County, 1990; North American—11 pounds, 4 ounces, Connecticut River, Massachusetts, 1986

Notes: The American Shad is a large shad very similar in appearance to the Hickory Shad. Both spawn in the same Florida waters and at about the same time. American Shad are common in the St. Johns River between Sanford and Melbourne from late December through March. Shad readily take small artificial lures and have become very popular with fly-fishermen. Shad are oily fish that are very good when smoked.

Description: deep, laterally compressed body; silvery blue back with white sides and belly; young fish have a dark spot on shoulder behind gill; small mouth; last rays of dorsal fin form a long thread

Similar Species: Alabama Shad (pg. 74), American Shad (pg. 76), Skipjack Herring (pg. 80)

Gizzard Shad	Alabama Shad	American Shad	Skipjack Herring
snout protruding over mouth, one dark spot on shoulder	one dark spot on shoulder, no jaw teeth, upper and lower jaw same length	mouth extends to back of eye, jaws even	lower jaw protruding over snout, no dark spot on shoulder, teeth on lower jaw

GIZZARD SHAD

Dorosoma cepedianum

Other Names: hickory, mud or jack shad

Habitat: large rivers, reservoirs, lakes, swamps and temporarily flooded pools; brackish and saline waters in coastal areas

Range: the St. Lawrence and Great Lakes, Mississippi, Atlantic and Gulf Slope drainages from Quebec to Mexico, south to central Florida; common in central Florida north through the Panhandle

Food: herbivorous filter feeder

Reproduction: spawning takes place in tributary streams and along lakeshores in early summer; schooling adults release eggs in open water without regard to mates

Average Size: 6 to 12 inches, 4 to 20 ounces

Records: State—none; North American—4 pounds, 12 ounces, Lake Oahe, South Dakota, 2006

Notes: The Gizzard Shad is a widespread, prolific fish that is best known as forage for popular game fish. It can overpopulate some lakes or impoundments and become the dominant fish, growing too large to be a prey species. The name "gizzard" refers to this shad's long, convoluted intestine that is often packed with sand. Though Gizzard Shad are a management problem at times, they form a valuable link in turning plankton into usable forage for larger game fish. Occasionally, larger Gizzard Shad are caught with hook and line, but they have little food value.

Description: deep, laterally compressed silver body; blue-green back; back color ends abruptly not shading into sides; no dark spots on the shoulder; sawtooth edge of sharply pointed scales along belly (scutes)

Similar Species: Alabama Shad (pg. 74), American Shad (pg. 76), Gizzard Shad (pg. 78)

Skipjack Herring	**Gizzard Shad**	**Alabama Shad**	**American Shad**
lower jaw pro-truding over snout, no dark spot on shoul-der, teeth on lower jaw	snout protrud-ing over mouth, one dark spot on shoulder	one dark spot on shoulder, no jaw teeth, upper and lower jaw same length	mouth extends to back of eye, jaws even

SKIPJACK HERRING

Alosa chrysochloris

Other Names: river herring, skipper

Habitat: clear water in large rivers, often at the mouth of tributary streams and below dams

Range: Gulf Coast waters from Texas to Florida, the Mississippi River and its large tributaries and impoundments; Florida Panhandle from Apalachicola River drainage west

Food: minnows and small fish, insects

Reproduction: little is known about spawning, but seems to spawn in early spring as individuals or in small schools in clear water near the mouth or tributary streams

Average Size: 12 to 16 inches, 1 to 2 pounds

Records: State—none; North American—3 pounds, 12 ounces, White Bear Lake, Tennessee, 1982

Notes: An agile fish, the Skipjack Herring was named for the spectacular leaps out of the water it often makes when pursuing prey. Skipjacks are fish of the big rivers and rarely enter smaller tributaries. They feed at the surface and prefer the clear, less turbid parts of the river. Skipjack Herring are only sought by a few anglers, but they readily take flies and small lures. On light tackle and in fast water, they can be one of the hardest fighting fish in Florida.

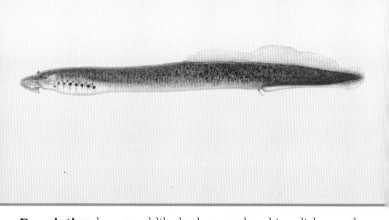

Description: brown eel-like body; round sucking-disk mouth; seven paired gill openings; dorsal fin long extending to tail; no paired fins

Similar Species: American Eel (pg. 62), Swamp Eel (pg. 162)

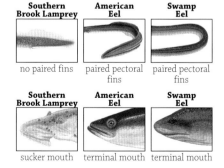

Southern Brook Lamprey	American Eel	Swamp Eel
no paired fins	paired pectoral fins	paired pectoral fins
Southern Brook Lamprey	American Eel	Swamp Eel
sucker mouth	terminal mouth	terminal mouth

SOUTHERN BROOK LAMPREY

Ichthyomyzon gagei

Other Names: brown or river lamprey

Habitat: juveniles live in the quiet pools of streams and rivers; some adults may move into brackish Gulf waters

Range: the Gulf drainage from Texas and Oklahoma north to Missouri, east to Tennessee, Georgia and Florida; from the Ochlockonee River west in the Florida Panhandle

Food: juvenile lampreys are bottom filter feeders in fresh water streams; adults are non-parasitic and do not feed

Reproduction: adult lampreys build a nest in the gravel of stream beds when water temperatures reach the mid 50s; adults die soon after spawning

Average Size: 6 to 12 inches

Records: none

Notes: Lampreys are primitive fish with skeletons made of cartilage and are some of earth's oldest vertebrates, with fossil records dating back 500 million years. Southern Brook Lampreys are not parasitic and do not feed in the adult form. The Sea Lamprey that devastated fisheries in the Great Lakes is parasitic and is present along Florida's Atlantic coast. In Florida, Sea Lampreys are a natural part of the environment and have little effect on native fish populations.

Description: side with eyes is light to dark brown with dark spots and blotches that do not have dark centers; light brown mottled fins; side without eyes is creamy white without spots; flat flounder-like body with eyes on top

Similar Species: Hogchoker (pg. 120)

Southern Flounder

dorsal fin extends to head

Hogchoker

dorsal fin extends to mouth

SOUTHERN FLOUNDER

Bothidae

Paralichthys lethostigma

Other Names: mud flounder, doormat, halibut

Habitat: marine areas; seasonally migrates up freshwater rivers, prefers open sand or silt bottom

Range: Atlantic coast from North Carolina to Mexico, Gulf coast from Florida to Texas; common in the St. Johns River on Florida's Atlantic coast, larger rivers from the Suwannee west through the Panhandle

Food: small fish

Reproduction: adults migrate offshore to spawn in late fall

Average Size: 12 to 24 inches; 2 to 6 pounds

Records: State—none; North American—20 pounds, 9 ounces, Nassau Sound, Florida, 1982

Notes: Flounders primarily inhabit the open ocean and estuaries but many migrate up large rivers during the summer. Flounders are regularly fished in the lower reaches of coastal rivers but often surprise fishermen when caught many miles from the ocean. Young flounders swim upright, with an eye on each side. As they mature, one eye moves; some to the left side of the body, some to the right side. Southern Flounders are a variety of flatfish and belong to the family of left-eye flounders—both eyes are on the left side of the body and adult fish lie flat on the right side of their body.

Description: silver to olive green back and sides; scales outlined, sides have a cross-hatched appearance; upturned mouth; dark bar under eye; rounded tail fin

Similar Species: Sailfin Molly (pg. 88)

Mosquitofish	Sailfin Molly	Mosquitofish	Sailfin Molly
dark bar under eye, slightly upturned mouth	no bar under eye, terminal mouth with protruding lips	small, rounded dorsal fin	large, angular dorsal fin

MOSQUITOFISH

Gambusia holbrooki

Other Names: mosquito or surface minnow

Habitat: surface of shallow, weedy backwaters with little current; lakes and swamps

Range: southeastern U.S., introduced worldwide; common throughout Florida

Food: insects, crustaceans and some plant material

Reproduction: gives birth to live young after internal fertilization; may produce several broods in a single season

Average Size: 2 to 3 inches

Records: none

Notes: There are few native livebearers in the U.S., but it is a well represented family in tropical and subtropical regions. Male Mosquitofish use their modified anal fin to transfer sperm to the much larger females. Females can store sperm up to ten months for later fertilization, then give birth to live young. Mosquitofish have been introduced worldwide to control mosquitoes but seem to be no better at it than native species. A hardy fish, Mosquitofish can withstand high temperatures, high salinity and low oxygen levels, making them well adapted to stagnant pools and swamps.

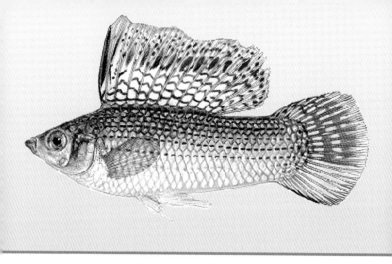

Description: dark olive green on back, lighter green on sides; 6 or 8 rows of dots on sides; brown dots on dorsal and tail fin; high angular dorsal fin almost as long as body; terminal mouth with protruding lips; breeding males iridescent blue body, orange on head and breast, orange spots on a purple tail fin

Similar Species: Mosquitofish (pg. 86)

Sailfin Molly	**Mosquitofish**	**Sailfin Molly**	**Mosquitofish**
no bar under eye, terminal mouth with protruding lips	dark bar under eye, slightly upturned mouth	large, angular dorsal fin	small, rounded dorsal fin

SAILFIN MOLLY

Mollienisia latipinna

Other Names: sailfin minnow

Habitat: weedy ponds, lakes, sloughs and low gradient streams; fresh and brackish water

Range: coastal North Carolina south to Vera Cruz, Mexico, Gulf states to the Rio Grande; common throughout Florida

Food: algae, small crustaceans, aquatic insects

Reproduction: gives birth to live young after internal fertilization; may produce several broods in a single season

Average Size: 2 to 3 inches

Records: none

Notes: A popular aquarium fish native to Central America, the Sailfin Molly is now well established from North Carolina to Texas. It is primarily a coastal and brackish water species, except in Florida where it is widespread. In some spring ponds and small lakes, Mollys can be very abundant. Like other members of the family, the anal fin in males is modified to transfer sperm to the much larger female. The sperm is stored for prolonged internal fertilization. The eggs develop in the female's body and the young are born alive.

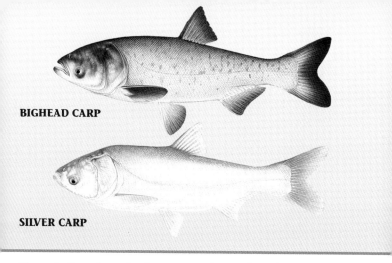

BIGHEAD CARP

SILVER CARP

Description: large body; upturned mouth without barbels; low-set eyes; small body scales; no scales on head

Similar Species: Common Carp (pg. 92), Grass Carp (pg. 94), Silver Carp

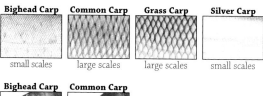

Bighead Carp	Common Carp	Grass Carp	Silver Carp
small scales	large scales	large scales	small scales

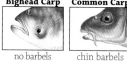

Bighead Carp	Common Carp
no barbels	chin barbels

BIGHEAD CARP
Hypophthalmichthys nobils

SILVER CARP *Hypophthalmichthys molitrix*

Other Names: Asian, Black, Bighead and Silver Carp

Habitat: large, warm rivers and connected lakes

Range: native to Asia, introduced in other parts of the world; in Florida, both species are restricted to aquaculture ponds, though Bighead Carp have been collected in Lake Okeechobee

Food: plankton, algae

Reproduction: spawns from late spring to early summer in warm, flowing water

Average Size: 16 to 22 inches, 5 to 50 pounds

Records: State—none; North American—90 pounds, Kirby Lake, Texas (Bighead Carp)

Notes: Bighead and Silver Carp were introduced into the United States to control unwanted algae growth in southern aquaculture ponds. They are important fish, farmed for food in many other countries. Both species have escaped from ponds in Arkansas and have had a devastating effect on the Mississippi, Ohio and Illinois Rivers. Both carp are voracious feeders that have the potential to disrupt the entire food chain. The Silver Carp, and to a lesser degree the Bighead Carp, makes high leaps from the water when frightened by boats.

Description: brassy yellow to golden brown or dark olive back and sides; white to yellow belly; two pairs of barbels near round, extendable mouth; red-tinged tail and anal fin; each scale has a dark spot at base and a dark margin

Similar Species: Bighead Carp (pg. 90), Grass Carp (pg. 94)

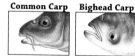

downturned mouth with barbels

upturned mouth lacks barbels

mouth upturned, no barbels

large scales

small scales

COMMON CARP

Cyprinus carpio

Cyprinidae

Other Names: German, European, mirror or leather carp, buglemouth

Habitat: warm, shallow, quiet, weedy waters of streams and lakes

Range: native to Asia, introduced throughout the world; common in the Apalachicola and Ochlockonee River basins in the Florida Panhandle

Food: opportunistic feeder, prefers insect larvae, crustaceans and mollusks, but will eat algae and some higher plants

Reproduction: spawns from late spring to early summer in very shallow water at stream and lake edges; very obvious when spawning with a great deal of splashing

Average Size: 16 to 18 inches, 5 to 20 pounds

Records: State—40 pounds, 8 ounces, Apalachicola River, Gadsden County, 1981; North American—57 pounds, 13 ounces, Tidal Basin, Washington D.C., 1983

Notes: One of the world's most important freshwater species, the fast-growing Common Carp provides sport and food for millions of people throughout its range. This Asian minnow was introduced into Europe in the twelfth century but didn't make it to North America until the 1800s. Carp are a highly prized sport fish in Europe but are despised by many U.S. anglers. Carp taken from clean water have a fine flavor. The meat is oily and bony and at its best when smoked.

Description: silver-gray head and sides with a golden-green sheen; fins grayish-green; large scales; eyes set in middle of head, terminal mouth; torpedo-shaped body not as deep as common carp

Similar Species: Common Carp (pg. 92)

Grass Carp	Common Carp
mouth upturned, no barbels, eye low on the head	downturned mouth with barbels, eye high on the head

GRASS CARP

Ctenopharyngodon idella

Cyprinidae

Other Names: white amur, silver or weed carp

Habitat: warm, shallow, quiet, weedy waters of streams and lakes

Range: native to Siberia's lower Amur River and northern China, now established in 20 countries; stocked in a few lakes and canals in Florida

Food: aquatic vegetation

Reproduction: spawns in streams where eggs are released and fertilized in a slow current; populations must be restocked as there is no natural reproduction

Average Size: 24 to 30 inches, 5 to 20 pounds

Records: State—none; North American—80 pounds, Lake Wedington, Arkansas, 2004

Notes: Grass Carp were first brought to the United States in 1961 by the U.S. Fish and Wildlife Service to control aquatic vegetation. Exposing Grass Carp eggs to heat results in triploid eggs (eggs with three sets of chromosomes instead of the normal two) and sterile fish. These Carp are now stocked in some Florida lakes in order to control aquatic vegetation. Grass Carp do not take bait readily, but a few are caught by anglers and are often large enough to put up a great fight. All hooked fish should be released to allow them to go about their job of weed control.

Description: back is gold to greenish-gold; sides golden with silver reflections; belly is yellowish-silver; deep slab-sided body; mouth angled up; long triangular-shaped head

Similar Species: Taillight Shiner (pg. 96)

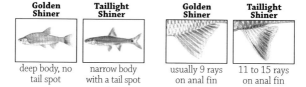

Golden Shiner	Taillight Shiner	Golden Shiner	Taillight Shiner
deep body, no tail spot	narrow body with a tail spot	usually 9 rays on anal fin	11 to 15 rays on anal fin

GOLDEN SHINER

Notemigonus crysoleucas

Cyprinidae

Other Names: bream, American bream, roach, American roach, butterfish, pond shiner

Habitat: clear, weedy ponds and quiet streams

Range: native to eastern U.S. south to Florida, introduced in the West; common throughout Florida

Food: planktonic crustaceans, aquatic insects, mollusks

Reproduction: extended midsummer spawning season; a female, attended by one or two males, spreads adhesive eggs over submerged vegetation; no parental care

Average Size: 3 to 7 inches

Records: none

Notes: Many of Florida's minnows are called shiners, and most are in the genus *Notropis*. Not all shiners are as flashy as the name indicates; some are dull and show almost no silver or gold on the sides. The Golden Shiner is a large, showy minnow that congregates in large schools, particularly when young. It is sometimes found in open water, but never far from vegetation. Golden Shiners are an important forage and baitfish; small ones are prized as bait for panfish, large ones for bass. They are commonly seined from the wild or propagated in fertilized ponds.

Description: silver to silver-gold body; dusky lines from gills
to tail; dark prominent spot at base of tail; scales have a
dark outline and a cross-hatched appearance; slightly protruding snout

Similar Species: Golden Shiner (pg. 96)

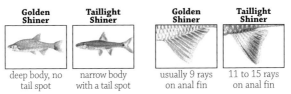

Golden Shiner	Taillight Shiner	Golden Shiner	Taillight Shiner
deep body, no tail spot	narrow body with a tail spot	usually 9 rays on anal fin	11 to 15 rays on anal fin

TAILLIGHT SHINER
Notemigonus maculatus

Other Names: lined or spottail shiner

Habitat: shallow backwaters, oxbow lakes and swamps with a muddy bottom and good vegetation

Range: Atlantic coast from Cape Fear through Florida to the Mississippi basin, north to Illinois; common throughout Florida

Food: planktonic crustaceans, aquatic insects, mollusks

Reproduction: extended spawning from spring through fall; adhesive eggs are spread over submerged vegetation; no parental care

Average Size: 3 to 7 inches

Records: none

Notes: There are many minnows in Florida called shiners, and most look very much alike and are hard to tell apart. The Taillight Shiner is one of the most widespread and abundant shiners and easy to identify. Its diamond-like scales, dark lateral line and distinctive "taillight" spot give it away. Taillight Shiners are reasonably hardy bait minnows, but they prefer to stay in the vegetation and are difficult to catch.

Description: green to tan above; small, dark saddles; dark green or brown mottling; many black speckles; slender, compressed body; fins clear and spotted

Similar Species: Banded Killifish (pg. 170)

Swamp Darter	Banded Killifish
two dorsal fins	single dorsal fin

SWAMP DARTER

Etheostoma fusiforme

Other Names: bog or weed darter

Habitat: sluggish streams, creeks and ditches with clear water and good vegetation

Range: coastal lowlands from Maine to Louisiana north through Tennessee and Missouri; common throughout Florida

Food: small aquatic invertebrates

Reproduction: in spring to early summer, males gather in breeding areas displaying little territoriality; females move from area to area spawning with several males; each sequence produces a few eggs that attach to the bottom

Average Size: 2 to 4 inches

Records: none

Notes: There are over 90 species of darters in North America and a dozen in Florida. Most are stream fish adapted to living among the rocks in fast currents, although some occupy lakes and sloughs. A small swim bladder allows darters to sink rapidly to the bottom after a "dart," preventing them from being swept away by the current. Darters are hard to see when they move, but they are easy to spot when "perched" on their pectoral fins. Breeding males can be very brightly colored but soon lose their color when kept in an aquarium.

Description: 6 to 9 olive green vertical bars on a yellow-brown background; two separate dorsal fins, the front all spines, the back soft rays; lower fins tinged yellow or orange, brighter in breeding males

Similar Species: Spotted Bass (pg. 140)

Yellow Perch   **Spotted Bass**

tall, hard-spined portions of dorsal fin not connected to soft rays

short, hard-spined portions of dorsal fin connected to soft rays

YELLOW PERCH
Perca flavescens

Other Names: ringed, striped or jack perch, green hornet

Habitat: lakes and streams; prefers clear, open water

Range: widely introduced throughout southern Canada and northern U.S.; introduced into the Apalachicola River in the Florida Panhandle

Food: minnows, insects, snails, leeches and crayfish

Reproduction: spawns at night in shallow, weedy areas when water temperatures reach 45 degrees; female drapes gelatinous ribbons of eggs on submerged vegetation

Average Size: 8 to 11 inches, 6 to 10 ounces

Records: State—none; North American—4 pounds, 3 ounces, Bordentown, New Jersey, 1865

Notes: Yellow Perch are a small, popular panfish native to north central U.S. that have now been introduced or spread to much of the southeast. Related to the Walleye, it has firm, mild-flavored, white flesh that is highly prized in the north. In the Great Lakes region, it is fished recreationally and commercially. In Florida, Yellow Perch are restricted to the Apalachicola River system where they enter Florida from Georgia. Yellow Perch can locally become very abundant and have a tendency to stunt, producing many fish too small for the pan.

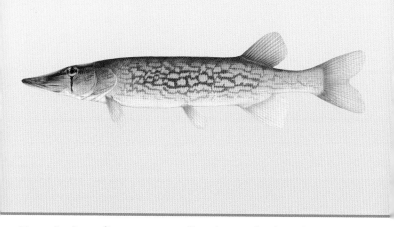

Description: olive green to yellow-brown back and sides; yellow-green chain-like markings on the sides; distinct dark teardrop below the eye; scales on the entire cheek and gill covers; fins almost clear

Similar Species: Redfin Pickerel (pg. 106)

Chain Pickerel

long, narrow head

Redfin Pickerel

short, broad head

CHAIN PICKEREL

Esox niger

Other Names: weed, jack or chain pike, jack pickerel

Habitat: shallow, weedy lakes and sluggish streams

Range: eastern United States from the Great Lakes and Maine to Florida west through Gulf states to Texas; common throughout Florida

Food: small fish, aquatic invertebrates

Reproduction: spawning takes place in April and May just as the ice goes out; adhesive eggs are deposited over shallow submerged vegetation and left to hatch with no parental care; occasionally spawns in fall with very low survival rate

Average Size: 18 to 24 inches, 1 to 3 pounds

Records: State—7 pounds, Lake Talquin, Okaloosa County, 2004; North American—9 pounds, 6 ounces, Homerville, Georgia, 1961

Notes: The Chain Pickerel is the largest of the pickerels and a respected game fish. Chain Pickerels frequent the outside edges of weedbeds and bite readily on minnow-imitating lures. When fished on light tackle or a fly rod, they are very good fighters. Chain Pickerels have a tendency to stunt when overcrowded, filling lakes and canals with half-pound "hammer handles."

Description: olive green to yellow-brown back and sides; sides have worm-like bars; distinct dark teardrop below eye; lower fins are tinged red, bright red in breeding males; scales on the entire cheek and gill cover

Similar Species: Chain Pickerel (pg. 104)

Redfin Pickerel

short, broad head

Chain Pickerel

long, narrow head

REDFIN PICKEREL

Esox americanus americanus

Other Names: red, mud, banded or little pickerel, red, grass, red-finned or mud pike

Habitat: shallow, weedy lakes and sluggish streams

Range: Atlantic states from Maine to Florida (east of Alleghenies) and east through the Gulf states; common in Florida north of Lake Okeechobee, uncommon in Everglades region

Food: small fish, aquatic invertebrates

Reproduction: spawns in early spring just as the ice goes out; adults enter flooded meadows and shallow bays to lay eggs in less than 2 feet of water; adhesive eggs are deposited over shallow, submerged vegetation; eggs are left to hatch with no parental care; similar spawning biology results in occasional hybridization with Chain Pickerel

Average Size: 10 to 12 inches, under 1 pound

Records: State—1 pounds, 1 ounce, New River, Bradford County, 1993; North American—2 pounds, 10 ounces, Lewis Lake, Georgia, 1982

Notes: The Redfin Pickerel is the smallest member of the pike family and is a common fish in well-vegetated lakes and streams along the Atlantic and throughout Florida. Redfin Pickerels are scrappy fighters on light tackle but are little more than a nuisance to anglers due to their small size. Redfin Pickerel do eat some small fish, but their diet consists mainly of larger invertebrates, including crayfish.

Description: females are a mottled olive brown, males have a lighter color; long, tubular body and mouth; no pelvic fins; long dorsal fin

Similar Species: none

GULF PIPEFISH
Syngnathus scouelli

Other Names: tube fish

Habitat: weedy coastal and marine waters; fresh water, including estuaries and rivers

Range: Gulf states through Central and South America to Brazil; common throughout Florida

Food: small zooplankton

Reproduction: females produce large eggs that are fertilized as they are placed in the male's brood pouch; young exit brood pouch when eggs hatch; males brood 1 to 3 clutches of eggs per season

Average Size: 6 inches

Records: none

Notes: The Gulf Pipefish is the only one of the 24 species of pipefish in North America that can be found in both salt water and fresh water. Freshwater Pipefish are most common in the larger coastal rivers. They are very abundant in the thickly vegetated parts of the St. Johns River. These interesting little fish are popular aquarium fish that readily breed in captivity. Like seahorses, the male pipefish brood the eggs in a special pouch.

Description: blue-gray back; silver-olive sides with 5 to 8 triangular-shaped dark gray-brown bars; deep body; protruding lip; breeding males have blue body with brassy cheeks, breast and belly; orange fins

Similar Species: Mosquitofish (pg. 86), Sailfin Molly (pg. 88)

Sheepshead Minnow

rounded dorsal and anal fin

Mosquitofish

small, rounded dorsal fin, pointed anal fin

Sailfin Molly

large, angular dorsal fin, pointed anal fin

Sheepshead Minnow

squared tail

Mosquitofish

rounded tail

SHEEPSHEAD MINNOW

Cyprinodon variegatus

Other Names: chubby, variegated minnow, sheepshead or broad killifish, sheepshead or Eustis pupfish

Habitat: quiet shallows of small streams or swamps with a muddy bottom; often found in open water near vegetation; frequents both fresh and brackish waters

Range: Maine to Yucatan and Venezuela, the Bahamas; common throughout Florida

Food: plant material, algae, detritus and aquatic insects

Reproduction: in spring through early summer, males construct and defend nest in open sandy areas; females lay adhesive eggs that attach to plants or stick on open sand

Average Size: 2 to 3 inches

Records: none

Notes: The Sheepshead Minnow is more common in brackish water over much of its range, but in Florida they are very abundant in both fresh and brackish water. Sheepshead Minnows found in lakes are not as thick-bodied as those found in brackish water and take on a much more elongated shape. This large, stout minnow is a popular aquarium and baitfish. Sheepshead Minnows are very hardy, even in marine conditions; they are one of the preferred baits when flounder fishing. When introduced to new habitat, Sheepshead Minnows readily hybridize with local pupfish species, often outcompeting and eliminating the native fish.

Description: dark olive green to brown body and head covered with small black specs; 10 or 11 black vertical bands on sides; black bands on dorsal, anal and tail fin; sunfish shape with rounded fins

Similar Species: Sheepshead Minnow (pg. 110)

Banded Pygmy Sunfish

small, elongated dorsal fin and anal fin

Sheepshead Minnow

rounded dorsal and anal fin

BANDED PYGMY SUNFISH

Elassomatidae

Elassoma zanatum

Other Names: little banded sunfish

Habitat: lakes, creeks and coastal swamps that are heavily vegetated with quiet waters and a soft bottom

Range: southeastern states from North Carolina to eastern Texas, the Mississippi River Valley through the Ohio basin to southern Illinois; common in central and northern Florida and through the Panhandle

Food: aquatic insect, zooplankton

Reproduction: males guard small territories but do not build a nest; eggs are laid in the vegetation and left with no parental care

Average Size: 1 to $1\frac{1}{2}$ inches

Records: none

Notes: Pygmy Sunfish are small, solitary fish that hide in dense vegetation. There are four Pygmy Sunfish found in Florida. The Banded Pygmy is the most common and wide-spread species. They look like tiny sunfish, and were once thought to be related to them, but they are not related and have been placed in their own family. Pygmy Sunfish adapt well to aquariums and the Everglades Pygmy Sunfish has long been popular in the European pet trade.

Description: sides bright silver to silver-green with a conspicuous light stripe; long, thin body; upturned mouth; 2 dorsal fins; tail deeply forked and pointed

Similar Species: Banded Killifish (pg. 170), Golden Shiner (pg. 96)

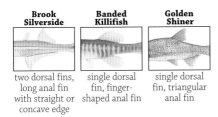

Brook Silverside	Banded Killifish	Golden Shiner
two dorsal fins, long anal fin with straight or concave edge	single dorsal fin, finger-shaped anal fin	single dorsal fin, triangular anal fin

114

BROOK SILVERSIDE

Labidesthes sicculus

Other Names: northern silverside, skipjack, friar

Habitat: surface of clear lakes; slack water of large streams

Range: Great Lake states south through central U.S. to Gulf states; common throughout Florida north of the Everglades

Food: aquatic and flying insects

Reproduction: spawns in late spring and early summer; eggs are laid in sticky strings that are attached to vegetation; most adults die after spawning

Average Size: 3 to 4 inches

Records: none

Notes: The Silverside is a member of a large family of primarily marine fish that are mostly tropical and subtropical. The Brook Silverside is a flashy fish that is often seen cruising near the lake surface in small schools. Its upturned mouth is an adaptation to surface feeding. It is not uncommon to see the Brook Silverside make spectacular leaps from the water, flying fish style, in pursuit of prey. Silversides have short life spans, lasting only 15 to 18 months.

Description: mottled brown to greenish-brown; cylindrical body; compressed head with a big mouth and sharp teeth; widely separated dorsal fins; tail fin rounded

Similar Species: Largemouth Bass (pg. 134)

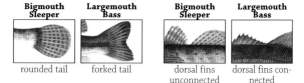

Bigmouth Sleeper	Largemouth Bass	Bigmouth Sleeper	Largemouth Bass
rounded tail	forked tail	dorsal fins unconnected	dorsal fins connected

BIGMOUTH SLEEPER

Gobiomorus dormitor

Other Names: rockfish, giant goby

Habitat: bottom dwellers in slow-moving streams and canals; coastal marine and brackish water

Range: south Florida to Dutch Guyana; in Florida, canals and coastal lagoons in Palm Beach, Broward and Dade Counties

Food: crustaceans and small fish

Reproduction: spawns in fresh or brackish water; adults build and guard nest eggs and young

Average Size: 10 to 18 inches, 8 ounces to 1 pound, 8 ounces

Records: none

Notes: Bigmouth Sleepers are nocturnal predators that hide among rocks or beside sunken logs in wait of prey. Sleepers are a surprise catch for anglers in the canals in southeast Florida. As sluggish feeders, they are not often caught by fishermen and almost never identified. They will bite on spinners and small plugs and are well thought of as food throughout their range. They prefer deeper water at the edge of weedbeds. Once common in Florida's coastal waters, they now seem to be on the decline, though they can be very common in some canals.

Description: dark brown back fading to lighter brown lower sides with irregular blotches; red-orange spot near base of tail; red eyes; large mouth with sharp teeth; long single dorsal fin; long anal fin

Similar Species: Bowfin (pg. 28)

Bullseye Snakehead	Bowfin	Bullseye Snakehead	Bowfin
pelvic fins near head	pelvic fins near middle of the body	long anal fin	short anal fin

BULLSEYE SNAKEHEAD

Channidae

Channa marulius

Other Names: cobra snakehead

Habitat: stagnant, shallow ponds and slow-moving streams with a muddy or weedy bottom

Range: native to Pakistan, Malaysia and southern China; canals and a few lakes in southeastern Florida

Food: fish, crayfish, frogs

Reproduction: spawns in the spring through early summer; builds nest in shallow weedbeds then aggressively guards nest and young

Average Size: 12 to 24 inches, 2 to 5 pounds

Records: none

Notes: The first Bullseye Snakehead was reported in Broward County in 2000. It is now established in several canals and lakes in southern Florida. A highly regarded sport- and food fish in its native range, it is another troublesome exotic for Florida. This air-breathing newcomer is well-adapted to the warm waters of southern Florida and will no doubt compete with native game fish. When pools begin to dry up, Snakeheads can slither through wet swamps in an attempt to find deeper water.

Description: color variable, side with eyes is a mottled light to dark brown or olive green with 6 to 8 dark bands across body; mottled fins; side without eyes is white; flat flounder-like body with eyes on top; tiny, rough scales giving body a hairy texture

Similar Species: Southern Flounder (pg. 84)

Hogchoker

dorsal fin extends to mouth

Southern Flounder

dorsal fin extends to head

HOGCHOKER
Trinectes maculatus

Other Names: Hogchoker Flounder

Habitat: marine to freshwater streams with open sand or a silt bottom

Range: the Atlantic coast from Massachusetts to Venezuela, Gulf coast from Florida to Texas; common in Florida's coastal rivers

Food: predator on small bottom crustaceans and aquatic insects

Reproduction: in early summer, adults return to marine estuaries to spawn; after hatching, larvae migrate up fresh water streams to mature; a 6 inch female may contain over 50,000 eggs

Average Size: 4 to 6 inches

Records: none

Notes: The Hogchoker is a plentiful coastal river fish that is most often encountered when caught in crab traps, fish traps or nets. Once encountered, Hogchokers leave a lasting impression, as Hogchokers quickly attach themselves to nets, buckets and fishermen. Its spiny scales and feathery fins give the Hogchoker a fuzzy feeling when handled. Hogchokers were reportedly named by early settlers after hogs choked after being fed the netted fish.

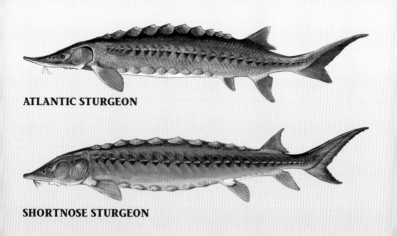

ATLANTIC STURGEON

SHORTNOSE STURGEON

Description: Atlantic—slate gray back and sides; snout long with a narrow mouth; two rows of scutes (bony plates) before anus; Shortnose—dark brown to black back and sides; snout short with large, wide mouth; both—five rows of scutes (bony plates), one on back, two on sides, two on bottom; tail is shark-like with the upper lobe much longer than lower

Similar Species: Shortnose Sturgeon

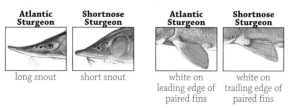

Atlantic Sturgeon	Shortnose Sturgeon	Atlantic Sturgeon	Shortnose Sturgeon
long snout	short snout	white on leading edge of paired fins	white on trailing edge of paired fins

122

Acipenseridae

ATLANTIC STURGEON
Acipenser oxyrhynchu

SHORTNOSE STURGEON *Acipenser brevirostrum*

Other Names: none

Habitat: large coastal rivers and estuaries

Range: Atlantic Sturgeon—Atlantic coast from Labrador to Florida, Gulf coast to Mississippi River; Shortnose Sturgeon—Atlantic coast from New Brunswick to Central Florida; both species have been collected on Florida's Atlantic coast

Food: snails, clams, crayfish and insects

Reproduction: migrates to brackish estuaries or rivers to spawn; thousands of eggs are laid over gravel bars in the current of large rivers; eggs fertilized a few at a time; sturgeon may reabsorb eggs if conditions are not suitable for spawning

Average Size: Atlantic—8 to 12 feet, 300 to 400 pounds; Shortnose—2 to 3 feet, 6 to 8 pounds

Records: none

Notes: Sturgeon are a primitive fish with a long history. Once commercially harvested for meat and caviar, now they are either threatened or endangered. Shortnosed Sturgeon are most likely to be found in the St. Johns River. The Atlantic sturgeon is extremely rare on Florida's east coast, but the gulf subspecies is still occasionally seen in Panhandle rivers. Sturgeons are threatened fish in Florida and should not be confused with sharks. Any sightings should be reported to the Fish and Game Department and if hooked every attempt made to return the fish to the water.

123

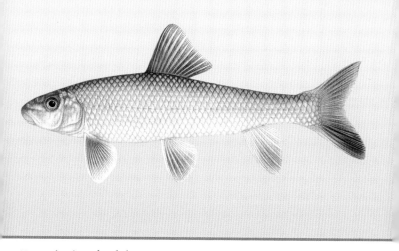

Description: back brassy-green to gold; silver to silver-green sides; off-white belly; distinctive tail, lower edge white with black band above; blunt nose and ventrally-placed sucker mouths; elongated body; sickle-shaped dorsal fin

Similar Species: Spotted Sucker (pg. 128)

Blacktail Redhorse

black stripe on lower lobe of tail

Spotted Sucker

no black on tail

124

BLACKTAIL REDHORSE

Moxostoma poecilurum

Other Names: golden sucker, golden or small-headed mullet

Habitat: clean streams and rivers with hard bottoms; occasionally, clear lakes or reservoirs with strong tributary streams

Range: Gulf slope from eastern Texas to the Choctawhatchee drainage in Florida, north up the Mississippi drainage to Tennessee; Florida Panhandle from Choctawhatchee River west

Food: aquatic insects, small crustaceans and plant matter

Reproduction: spawns from late May through June when the water temperature reaches the low 60s; adults migrate into small tributary streams to lay eggs on shallow gravel bars in the current near deep water pools

Average Size: 10 to 18 inches, 1 to 2 pounds

Records: State—none; North American—14 pounds, 4 ounces, Pickwick Lake, Alabama, 1995

Notes: There are three redhorse species in Florida—the River, Grayfin and Blacktail. All are "sucker type fish" and rather similar in appearance and hard to tell apart. They may all look alike, but each is a separate species and occupies its own niche in Florida waters. They are cleanwater fish and very susceptible to increased turbidity and pollutants. Redhorses are more commonly found in streams but do inhabit a few impoundments. Though not important sport fish, they are a fairly common catch of river anglers. They fight well on light tackle and, though bony, have a good flavor when smoked.

125

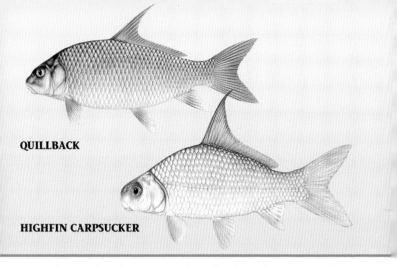

QUILLBACK

HIGHFIN CARPSUCKER

Description: bright silver back and sides, often with yellow tinge; fins clear; deep body with round, blunt head; leading edge of dorsal fin extends into a large, arching "quill"

Similar Species: Common Carp (pg. 92)

Quillback	Highfin Carpsucker	Common Carp
chin lacks barbels, no knob on lip	no barbels on chin, knob in middle of lower lip	barbels on chin

QUILLBACK *Carpiodes cyprinus*
HIGHFIN CARPSUCKER *Carpiodes velifer*

Other Names: silver carp, carpsucker, lake quillback

Habitat: slow-flowing streams and rivers; backwaters and lakes, particularly areas with soft bottoms

Range: south-central Canada through the Great Lakes to the eastern U.S., south through the Mississippi drainage to the Gulf; in Florida, present in the western Panhandle

Food: insects, plant matter, decaying bottom material

Reproduction: spawns in late spring through early summer in tributaries or lake shallows; eggs are deposited in open areas over sand or mud bottom

Average Size: 12 to 14 inches, 1 to 3 pounds

Records: Quillback, State—none; North American—8 pounds, 13 ounces, Lake Winnebago, Wisconsin, 2003; Highfin, none

Notes: In Florida, the Quillback and Highfin are the only representatives of the four North American fish known as carpsuckers. Both look very much alike and prefer medium to large rivers with clean water and soft bottoms. Even through they are restricted to the western Panhandle, they can be a locally very common fish. They are schooling fish that filter feed along the bottom. Not often sought by anglers, they readily take wet flies and can be good fighters when caught on light tackle. The flesh is white and very flavorful, though bony.

Description: olive brown back; yellow to olive sides; creamy yellow belly; scales have distinct dark edges producing a cross-hatched appearance; sucker mouth; breeding males have three large tubercles on each side of the head; young have dark stripe from head to tail

Similar Species: Golden Shiner (pg. 96)

sucker mouth   terminal mouth

LAKE CHUBSUCKER

Erimyzon sucetta

Other Names: chubsucker, sweet or yellow sucker, pin sucker, pin minnow

Habitat: sluggish pools of small to midsized streams and clear lakes with good vegetation growth

Range: Gulf and Atlantic coast from north Texas to Maine, the Mississippi River drainage north to the southern Great Lakes; statewide in Florida

Food: small crustaceans and aquatic insects

Reproduction: spawns any time water temperatures are in the 60s; a shallow nest is excavated in the sand or gravel of small tributary streams; males aggressively defend breeding territories around nest; eggs and young are not guarded

Average Size: 8 to 10 inches

Records: none

Notes: The Lake Chubsucker is one of the most important forage fish in many small Florida lakes and streams. Chubsuckers are very prolific and even small numbers of breeding adults produce large numbers of fry for game fish. They survive well on a hook and in bait pails, making them ideal large bait minnows. Chubsuckers readily take a worm on a hook and can provide great sport for young kids spending a day on the creek.

Description: dark olive back; silver sides; each scale has dark spot producing parallel rows of spots down sides; white belly; sucker mouth; long, cylindrical body; breeding males develop lateral bands, lower bands are chocolate-gray, middle bands are grayish-pink, upper bands are dark lavender

Similar Species: Blacktail Redhorse (pg. 124)

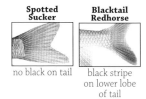

Spotted Sucker
no black on tail

Blacktail Redhorse
black stripe on lower lobe of tail

SPOTTED SUCKER

Minytrema melanops

Other Names: corncob, striped, speckled sucker, spotted redhorse

Habitat: sluggish pools of large to midsized streams and rivers with good vegetation

Range: Gulf states from Texas to Florida, the Mississippi River drainage north to the southern Great Lakes; common in Florida Panhandle through the Suwannee River drainage

Food: small crustaceans and aquatic insects

Reproduction: long spawning season any time water temperatures are in the 60s; males aggressively defend territories in shallow riffles; eggs and young are left unattended

Average Size: 8 to 10 inches, 8 ounces to 1 pound

Records: State—none; North American—1 pound, 6 ounces, Catfish Creek, Texas, 2002

Notes: Spotted Suckers are one of the most prolific and important forage fish in northern Florida streams. Spotted Suckers, like other species in the family, require clean, high-quality water with little siltation. As such, they are good indicators of stream quality. Suckers are a common large baitfish, but an uncommon sport fish. For sport they are mostly sought during spawning runs when they are netted or speared. The flesh is oily and bony, but firm and white. Suckers are very popular in the north where they are smoked, but less popular in the south.

131

Description: gray body covered with a row of hard, bony plates; head is dark gold and covered with dark worm-like marks; sucker-type mouth under head; large dorsal fin; upper tail lobe long and pointed

Similar Species: other armored catfish in genus *Ptergoplichthys* and *Hypostomus*

Loricariidae

SAILFIN CATFISH

Clarias batrachus

Other Names: Orinoco sailfin, armored or suckermouth
catfish, butterfly pleco, hypostomus

Habitat: slow-moving streams and canals; shallow lakes and
ponds

Range: Amazon River basin in South America, established in
Texas and Florida; widespread in central and south Florida

Food: algae, detritus and small crustaceans

Reproduction: adhesive eggs are laid in burrows or natural
cavities; eggs and young are guarded by adults

Average Size: 10 to 15 inches, 1 pound to 1 pound, 8 ounces

Records: none

Notes: While several armored catfish have been collected or
are established in Florida, the Sailfin Catfish is the only
one that is widespread. Most are small and hard to tell apart.
All have "sucker-type mouths" that are used to attach to
rocks while feeding on algae. The smaller species are popular
aquarium fish that help in cleaning algae from tank walls.
Sailfin Catfish are not often attracted to baited hooks but
are sometimes caught while fishing on the bottom. They
reach 2 or 3 pounds and have good flavor but are impos-
sible to clean. They are best baked in the "shell" and then
cracked open to eat.

pterygoplichthys
multiradiatus

Description: dark green back; a dark lateral band; belly white to gray; large forward-facing mouth; lower jaw extends to rear margin of eye

Similar Species: Shoal Bass (pg. 138), Spotted Bass (pg. 140), Suwannee Bass (pg. 142)

Largemouth Bass	Shoal Bass	Spotted Bass	Suwannee Bass
mouth extends past eye	mouth doesn't extend past eye	mouth doesn't extend past eye	mouth doesn't extend past eye

Largemouth Bass	Shoal Bass	Spotted Bass	Suwannee Bass
notched dorsals, no scales on base of dorsal/anal fins	heavily notched dorsals, scales on base of dorsal/anal fins	shallowly notched dorsals with scales at base of dorsal/anal fins	shallowly notched dorsals, scales on base of dorsal/anal fins

LARGEMOUTH BASS

Micropterus salmoides

Centrarchidae

Other Names: black, bayou, green or slough bass, green trout

Habitat: shallow, fertile, weedy lakes and river backwaters; weedy bays and extensive weedbeds of large lakes

Range: native to peninsular Florida, now stocked in other states; common throughout Florida

Food: small fish, frogs, insects, crayfish

Reproduction: spawns when water temperatures reach 60 degrees; male builds a nest in small clearings in weedbeds 2 to 8 feet deep, then guard nest and fry until the "brood swarm" disperses

Average Size: 12 to 20 inches, 1 to 5 pounds

Records: State—17 pounds, 4 ounces, unnamed lake, Polk County, 1986; North American—22 pounds, 4 ounces, Montgomery Lake, Georgia, 1932

Notes: The Largemouth Bass is the most sought after game fish in North America. This denizen of the weedbeds is a voracious carnivore and eats anything that is alive and will fit into its mouth. The Florida Largemouth is a slightly larger subspecies of the Northern Largemouth Bass. There is a great deal of interbreeding between the two subspecies throughout Florida, so it can be difficult to tell which subspecies one has caught. Bass can be found in most of Florida's waters including slightly salty, brackish waters.

Description: dark green to black with greenish-brown sides and dark bars; red eye; dark stripes extending from eye; lower jaw extends to front of eye; shallow notch between hard/soft dorsal fins; scales on base of dorsal and anal fin

Similar Species: Largemouth Bass (pg. 134), Shoal Bass (pg. 138), Spotted Bass (pg. 140)

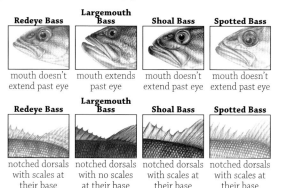

Redeye Bass	Largemouth Bass	Shoal Bass	Spotted Bass
mouth doesn't extend past eye	mouth extends past eye	mouth doesn't extend past eye	mouth doesn't extend past eye

Redeye Bass	Largemouth Bass	Shoal Bass	Spotted Bass
notched dorsals with scales at their base	notched dorsals with no scales at their base	notched dorsals with scales at their base	notched dorsals with scales at their base

REDEYE BASS

Micropterus coosae

Centrarchidae

Other Names: Flint River bass

Habitat: rocky shallows in rivers and small streams

Range: Alabama, Georgia and South Carolina; rare, if at all, in the Florida Panhandle

Food: small fish, frogs, insects and crayfish

Reproduction: ascends small tributary streams to spawn when water temperatures reach 60 degrees; males build nest, then guard the nest and fry; does not reproduce well in waters without a current

Average Size: 10 to 18 inches, 2 to 4 pounds

Records: State—7 pounds, 13 ounces, Gadsden County, 1989; North American—8 pounds, 3 ounces, Flint River, Georgia, 1977

Notes: For many years, all the bass in Florida's Panhandle with red eyes were considered to be the Redeye Bass, *M. coosae*. In the late '90s it was determined that the Florida bass were a different species, the Shoal Bass, *M. cataractae,* and there were few, if any, Redeye Bass in Florida. There is even some controversy regarding the identification of the Florida state record Redeye Bass. It may have been mis-identified, and in reality might be a Shoal Bass. Needless to say, both species are very similar and hard to tell apart.

Description: dark green back; greenish sides with dark blotches; dark spot on gill and base of tail; red eye; dark stripes extend from eye; lower jaw extends to front of eye; shallow notch between dorsal fins with scales at their base

Similar Species: Largemouth Bass (pg. 134), Redeye Bass (pg. 136), Spotted Bass (pg. 140)

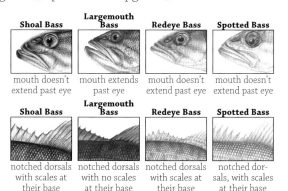

Shoal Bass	Largemouth Bass	Redeye Bass	Spotted Bass
mouth doesn't extend past eye	mouth extends past eye	mouth doesn't extend past eye	mouth doesn't extend past eye
Shoal Bass	Largemouth Bass	Redeye Bass	Spotted Bass
notched dorsals with scales at their base	notched dorsals with no scales at their base	notched dorsals with scales at their base	notched dorsals, with scales at their base

SHOAL BASS

Micropterus cataractae

Other Names: Flint River bass

Habitat: rocky shallows in rivers and small streams

Range: Florida Panhandle and possibly southern Georgia; in Florida, the Apalachicola, Chipola, Chattahoochee and Flint River drainages

Food: small fish, frogs, insects and crayfish

Reproduction: ascends small tributary streams to spawn when water temperatures reach 60 degrees; males build nest then guard the nest and fry

Average Size: 10 to 18 inches, 2 to 4 pounds

Records: State—7 pounds, 13 ounces, Apalachicola River, 1989; North American—8 pounds, 3 ounces, Flint River, Georgia, 1977

Notes: For a long time, Shoal Bass were considered to be a subspecies of the Redeye Bass and there is still a great deal of confusion concerning the two. In the late '90s, Shoal Bass were designated a separate species. It is now thought that the Shoal Bass is the common, fastwater river bass in northern Florida and there are few, if any, Redeye Bass. The surest way to differentiate between the two species is by counting scales. Shoal Bass have 18 to 19 scale rows below the lateral line and 72 to 77 scales in the lateral line. Redeye Bass have 16 to 17 scale rows below the lateral line and 67 to 72 scales in the lateral line.

Description: dark green back fading to lighter green sides; diamond shaped blotches form a dark stripe on side; dark spots above stripe; light spots on base of each scale below stripe; dark lines extend from the reddish eye

Similar Species: Largemouth Bass (pg. 134), Shoal Bass (pg. 138)

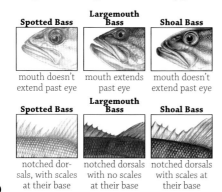

Spotted Bass	Largemouth Bass	Shoal Bass
mouth doesn't extend past eye	mouth extends past eye	mouth doesn't extend past eye
notched dorsals, with scales at their base	notched dorsals with no scales at their base	notched dorsals with scales at their base

SPOTTED BASS

Micropterus punctulatus

Other Names: Kentucky, Speckled or Yellow Bass, Spottys

Habitat: deeper, silted pools in sluggish, medium to large streams; larger lakes and reservoirs

Range: the Ohio and Mississippi drainage in the southern U.S. from Florida to Texas; Florida's Panhandle streams, primarily west of the Choctawhatchee River

Food: small fish and crayfish

Reproduction: males build nest in open gravel beds 3 to 4 feet deep from May to June when water temperatures reach mid to high 60s; males aggressively guard the nest and young

Average Size: 8 to 18 inches, 8 ounces to 2 pounds

Records: State—3 pounds, 12 ounces, Apalachicola River, Gadsden County, 1993; North American—10 pounds, 4 ounces, Pine Flat Lake, California, 2001

Notes: This bass is primarily a stream fish but has done well in large impoundments. It is rarely found in natural lakes. Spotted Bass are similar in habit to Shoal Bass. Spotted and Shoal Bass seek out steam riffles, whereas Largemouths prefer the edges of weedbeds and slower, deep pools. In reservoirs, Spotted Bass seek deeper water than Largemouth Bass, often near the bottom on the outside edges of deep weedbeds or rock ledges. Spotted Bass are smaller than Largemouth Bass but are very good fighters on light tackle and somewhat better flavored.

141

Description: dark green back; greenish-brown sides with dark blotches; lower sides and pectoral fins are turquoise; red eye; lower jaw extends to eye; shallow notch between hard/soft dorsal fins; scales on base of dorsal or anal fin

Similar Species: Largemouth Bass (pg. 134), Shoal Bass (pg. 138), Spotted Bass (pg. 140)

Suwannee Bass	Largemouth Bass	Shoal Bass	Spotted Bass
mouth doesn't extend past eye	mouth extends past eye	mouth doesn't extend past eye	mouth doesn't extend past eye
Suwannee Bass	**Largemouth Bass**	**Shoal Bass**	**Spotted Bass**

notched dorsals with scales at their base	notched dorsals with no scales at their base	notched dorsals with scales at their base	notch dorsals with scales at their base

SUWANNEE BASS

Micropterus notius

Other Names: blue belly, river or riffle bass

Habitat: rocky riffles of medium to large rivers

Range: restricted to northern Florida and southern Georgia; Ochlockonee River to the Suwannee Rivers in northwest Florida, introduced into the Aucilla/Wacissa system

Food: small fish, frogs, insects and crayfish

Reproduction: spawns when water temperatures reach 60 degrees; males build nest in the quiet, weedy water along stream edges; males guard the nest and fry

Average Size: 8 to 10 inches, 1 to 2 pounds

Records: State—3 pounds, 14 ounces, Suwannee River, Gilchrist County, 1985 (not recorded as NA record); North American—3 pounds, 9 ounces, Ochlockonee River, Georgia, 1984

Notes: Suwannee Bass are a small bass that rarely exceed 12 inches. They are closely related to Redeye and Spotted Bass. Suwannee Bass are river fish and do not naturally occur in lakes. Native to the Suwannee River drainage, they have been introduced into the Aucilla/Wacissa system in recent years. Though small, they are hard fighters in fast water and prized by fly-fishermen fishing small tributaries of the Suwannee River.

Description: black to olive back; silver sides with dark green to black blotches; back more arched and depression above eye more pronounced than in the White Crappie

Similar Species: Jaguar Guapote (pg. 50)

Black Crappie	Jaguar Guapote	Black Crappie	Jaguar Guapote
large, fragile mouth without teeth, rounded anal and dorsal fin	large, robust mouth with teeth, pointed anal and dorsal fin	pointed anal and dorsal fins	rounded anal and dorsal fins

BLACK CRAPPIE

Centrarchidae

Pomoxis nigromaculatus

Other Names: speckled perch, speck, papermouth

Habitat: quiet, clear water of streams and midsized lakes; often associated with vegetation but may roam deep, open basins and flats, particularly during winter

Range: southern Manitoba through the Atlantic and south-eastern states, introduced but not common in the West; common throughout Florida except in the Keys

Food: small fish, aquatic insects, zooplankton

Reproduction: spawns in shallow weedbeds from early spring when water temperatures reach the high 50s; male builds circular nest in fine gravel or sand and then guards the eggs and young until fry begin feeding

Average Size: 7 to 12 inches, 8 ounces to 1 pound

Records: State—3 pounds, 13 ounces, Lake Talquin, Gadsden County, 1992; North American—6 pounds, Westwego Canal, Louisiana, 1969

Notes: The Black Crappie is the most widespread crappie in North America and is found in most Florida lakes and slow-moving streams that have clear water and good vegetative growth. Crappies are a schooling fish that, when not spawning, are often found suspended in deeper water. They nest in colonies and frequently gather in large feeding schools in winter. Black Crappies are sought for their sweet-tasting white fillets, but not their fighting ability.

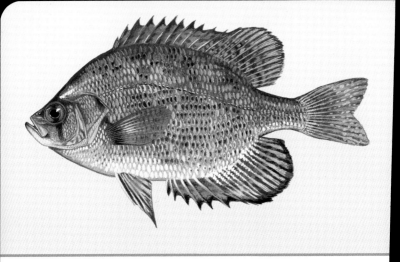

Description: olive green to silver-green back and sides; longitudinal stripes of brown spots on sides; dark wedge shaped bar under eye; latterly compressed body; anal and dorsal fin nearly equal length; dark spot on dorsal fin of young fish; small mouth

Similar Species: Black Crappie (pg. 144)

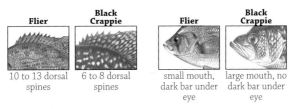

Flier	Black Crappie	Flier	Black Crappie
10 to 13 dorsal spines	6 to 8 dorsal spines	small mouth, dark bar under eye	large mouth, no dark bar under eye

FLIER

Centrarchus macropterus

Other Names: spotfin, silver, round or swamp sunfish

Habitat: quiet, weedy waters with a soft bottom in lakes, creeks and coastal swamps

Range: coastal states from Virginia to eastern Texas, the Mississippi Valley through the Ohio Valley to Southern Illinois and Indiana; common in central and northern Florida

Food: aquatic insects, zooplankton, small fish

Reproduction: nests in late spring or early summer in dense vegetation; nests are solitary or in small groups; males guard nest and young

Average Size: 4 to 6 inches, 4 ounces

Records: State—1 pound, 1 ounce, Lake Iamonia, Leon County, 1992; North American—1 pound, 2 ounces, Pope's Pond, Georgia, 1995

Notes: Fliers are small sunfish native to northern Florida that can withstand low oxygen and more acidity than most other sunfish. They are very common in still, swampy water. Rarely larger than 6 inches long, Fliers are too small to be an important panfish, but they readily bite and can be proficient bait robbers. When large enough to eat, Fliers have flaky, white flesh and a fine flavor. Fliers are predators of mosquito larvae, and small ones should be carefully returned to the water to help with mosquito control.

Description: dark olive to green on back, blending to silver-gray, copper, orange, purple or brown on sides; 5 to 9 dark vertical bars on sides that fade with age; yellow belly and copper breast; large, dark gill spot; dark spot on dorsal fin

Similar Species: Green Sunfish (pg. 150), Redbreast Sunfish (pg. 154)

Bluegill	**Green Sunfish**	**Redbreast Sunfish**
dark gill spot on rounded gill flap	prominent light margin on rounded gill spot	long, narrow gill flap

Bluegill	**Green Sunfish**
small mouth	large mouth

148

BLUEGILL

Lepomis macrochirus

Other Names: bream, sun perch, blue sunfish, copperbelly, strawberry bass

Habitat: medium to large streams and most lakes with weedy bays or shorelines

Range: southern Canada through the southern states into Mexico; native and common throughout Florida

Food: aquatic insects, snails, small fish

Reproduction: spawns from late May to early August when water temperatures reach the high 60s to low 80s; male builds a nest in shallow, sparse vegetation in a colony of up to 50 other nests; male guards nest and fry

Average Size: 6 to 9 inches, 5 to 8 ounces

Records: State—2 pounds, 15 ounces, Crystal Lake, Washington County, 1989; North American—4 pounds, 12 ounces, Ketona Lake, Alabama, 1950

Notes: Bluegills are the most popular panfish in Florida and throughout the United States. Bluegills have small mouths and feed mostly on insects and small fish, often at the surface. Bluegills prefer deep weedbeds at the edge of open water. Many lakes have large populations of hybrid sunfish, crosses between Bluegills and other sunfish. Bluegills are thought by many to be one of the most delicious freshwater fish. Painted Bream are not a separate species, but a strain of Bluegill with a pink throat and dark blotches on the sides.

Description: dark green back with dark olive to bluish sides; yellow to cream belly; scales flecked with yellow, producing a brassy appearance; dark gill spot with light margin; large mouth and thick lips

Similar Species: Bluegill (pg. 148), Redear Sunfish (pg. 156)

Green Sunfish

prominent light margin on rounded gill spot

Bluegill

round gill spot with clear margin

Redear Sunfish

red-orange margin on gill spot

Green Sunfish

blue stripes on head

Redear Sunfish

no blue stripes on head

GREEN SUNFISH
Lepomis cyanellus

Other Names: green perch, sand bass

Habitat: warm, weedy, shallow lakes and the backwaters of slow-moving streams

Range: most of the United States into Mexico, excluding most of Florida and the Rocky Mountains; restricted in Florida to the Apalachicola River drainage and west

Food: aquatic insects, small crustaceans, fish

Reproduction: male builds a nest in less than a foot of weedy water when temperatures reach 60 to 80 degrees; may produce two broods per year; male guards nest and fans eggs until hatching

Average Size: 4 to 6 inches, less than 8 ounces

Records: State—none; North American—2 pounds, 2 ounces, Stockton Lake, Missouri, 1971

Notes: Green Sunfish are often mistaken for Bluegills but are not as deep-bodied and prefer shallower weedbeds. Very tolerant of turbid water and low oxygen levels, they thrive in warm, weedy lakes and backwaters. Green Sunfish stunt easily, filling some lakes with 3-inch-long "potato chips." Green Sunfish sometimes hybridize with other sunfish, producing large, aggressive offspring, but in the end these crosses result in poor panfish populations. Green Sunfish are not found in most of Florida and their presence would harm other panfish populations. All possible care should be taken not to spread this sunfish to the rest of Florida.

Description: dark greenish-blue back; sides light green flecked with blue or yellow; belly and chest bright orange to pale yellow; gill flap tapers into a long, black finger with red margin

Similar Species: Redear Sunfish (pg. 156)

Longear Sunfish
blue-green bands on side of head

Redear Sunfish
solid green to bronze head

Longear Sunfish
dark spots on dorsal fin

Redear Sunfish
no spots on dorsal fin

LONGEAR SUNFISH

Lepomis magalotis

Other Names: Great Lakes longear, blue and orange sunfish, red perch, longear bream

Habitat: clear, moderately weedy, slow-moving, shallow streams and quiet, clear lakes

Range: central states north to Quebec, east to the Appalachian Mountains and as far south as the Gulf of Mexico, introduced into some western states; Florida's western Panhandle

Food: small insects, crustaceans and fish

Reproduction: males build and guard nest on shallow gravel beds when water temperatures reach the mid-70s

Average Size: 3 to 6 inches, ⅓ pound

Records: State—none; North American—1 pound, 12 ounces, Big Round Lake, New Mexico

Notes: Longears are highly-colored, secretive little sunfish that prefer clear, slow-moving shallow streams, but do inhabit some clean Florida lakes. This southern species is not widespread in Florida but can be very abundant locally. These sunfish require clean water and are disappearing from many streams due to increased siltation due to agriculture. Longears feed on the surface more than other sunfish and are popular with fly fishermen. There is some hybridization between Longears and other sunfish.

Description: dark olive green back; olive sides; gray-white belly; bright yellow-orange breast; gill flap long, black and narrower than the eye; tail slightly forked

Similar Species: Bluegill (pg. 148), Redear Sunfish (pg. 156)

Redbreast Sunfish	Bluegill	Redear Sunfish
long, narrow dark gill flap	round gill spot with clear margin	red-orange margin on gill spot

REDBREAST SUNFISH

Lepomis auritus

Other Names: yellow belly or longear sunfish, sun perch, redbreast bream

Habitat: rocky riffles in streams with some current; occasionally lakes or reservoirs

Range: the Atlantic drainage from southern New York to Florida; common in central and northern Florida, the dominant sunfish from the Suwannee River through the Panhandle to the Ochlockonee River

Food: aquatic insects, crustaceans, small fish

Reproduction: spawns in May and June when water temperatures reach the high 60s; male builds small, round nest in weedbeds away from the current; male defends nest

Average Size: 4 to 8 inches, 4 ounces to 8 ounces

Records: State—2 pounds, 1 ounce, Suwannee River, Gilchrist County, 1988; North American—2 pounds, 1 ounce, Suwannee River, Florida, 1988

Notes: This is a common, small to medium sized sunfish native to the Atlantic drainage east of the Alleghenies. They prefer streams but are frequently found in reservoirs and impoundment lakes. Redbreast Sunfish are often found around rocks, logs or undercut banks near moving water. Redbreasts are very popular sunfish in some areas. Slightly more nocturnal than other sunfish, they bite aggressively on small artificial lures and live bait both day and night.

Description: back and sides bronze to dark green, fading to light green; sides have faint vertical bars and small spots; gill flap short with dark spot and red margin in males; breast yellow or orange

Similar Species: Bluegill (pg. 148), Redbreast Sunfish (pg. 154)

Redear Sunfish	**Bluegill**	**Redbreast Sunfish**
red-orange margin on gill spot	round gill spot with clear margin	long, narrow dark gill flap

REDEAR SUNFISH

Centrarchidae

Lepomis microlophus

Other Names: shellcracker, stumpknocker, yellow bream

Habitat: congregates around stumps and logs in low to moderate vegetation in lakes and swamps and large quiet streams; prefers sand or gravel bottoms; frequents brackish water

Range: the northern Midwest through the southern states, introduced into the northern and western states; common throughout Florida

Food: mollusks

Reproduction: males build and guard nest in shallow vegetated water in spring when water temperatures reach high 60s; may produce second brood well into summer

Average Size: 8 to 10 inches, 8 ounces to 1 pound

Records: State—4 pounds, 14 ounces, Merritt's Mill Pond, Jackson County, 1986; North America—5 pounds, 7.5 ounces, Diversion Canal, South Carolina, 1998

Notes: The Redear is a large, highly regarded sunfish from the South that has now been introduced into many northern states. Redears are often found in dense vegetation where they feed on snails attached to plant stems. This makes them somewhat harder to locate and catch than other sunfish. Redears are more tolerant of brackish water than other sunfish and are often found along the deep water edges of salt marshes and coastal stream mouths. Redears are one the most popular sunfish in peninsular Florida, particularly south of Lake Okeechobee.

Description: olive green to black back; scales on the sides each have a dark spot at base producing regular rows of spots; lower sides and belly dull red to reddish-brown; plain dark gill spot with light margin

Similar Species: Bluegill (pg. 148), Redear Sunfish (pg. 156)

Spotted Sunfish

no blotch near rear base of dorsal fin

Bluegill

blotch near rear base of dorsal fin

Spotted Sunfish

rounded pectoral fin

Redear Sunfish

pointed pectoral fin

SPOTTED SUNFISH

Lepomis punctatus

Other Names: stumpknocker, spotted bream, bream

Habitat: slow-moving, weedy streams and rivers with hard bottoms

Range: South Carolina south to Florida, west to Texas, north up the Mississippi River basin to Illinois; common in north and central peninsula Florida and the eastern Panhandle

Food: aquatic insects and small fish

Reproduction: males build and guard a solitary nest in shallow, well-vegetated water in spring when water temperatures reach the high 60s; males guard nest very aggressively

Average Size: 4 to 6 inches, 4 ounces

Records: State—13 ounces, Suwannee River, Columbia County, 1984; North America—2 pounds, 11 ounces, Hall's Lake, Georgia, 1985 (IGFA)

Notes: The Spotted Sunfish is most often found in weedy, slow-moving streams. In many such streams it is the predominant sunfish. Spotted Sunfish have a tendency to feed on, or near, the bottom more than other sunfish. However, Spotted Sunfish are aggressive feeders, and though often too small to keep, they can be locally very abundant and a persistent bait robber in some streams.

Description: back greenish-gray to brown; faint vertical bands; stout body; large mouth; red eyes; 3-5 reddish-brown streaks near eyes; dark spots on dorsal/anal fins

Similar Species: Bluegill (pg. 148), Green Sunfish (pg. 150), Redear (pg. 156)

Warmouth

jaw extends at least to middle of eye

Bluegill

small mouth doesn't extend to eye

Green Sunfish

jaw doesn't extend to middle of eye

Warmouth

light margin on gill spot

Redear Sunfish

red/orange margin on gill spot

Rock Bass

dark gill spot, light margin

WARMOUTH

Lepomis gulosus

Other Names: goggle eye, widemouth sunfish, stumpknocker, weed bass

Habitat: heavy weeds in turbid lakes, swamps and slow-moving streams

Range: southern U.S. from Texas to Florida north to the southern Great Lakes region; common throughout Florida

Food: prefers crayfish, but eats aquatic insects and small fish

Reproduction: solitary nesters when water temperatures reach high 60s to 70s; males build nest in coarse gravel in submerged vegetation less than 3 feet deep; males guard eggs and fry

Average Size: 11 inches, 8 to 12 ounces

Records: State—2 pounds, 7 ounces, Yellow River, Okaloosa County, 1985; North American—2 pounds, 7 ounces, Yellow River, Florida, 1985

Notes: This secretive sunfish is common in Florida's shallow lakes and swamps. Warmouths are solitary, aggressive sight-feeders often found around rocks and submerged stumps when not hiding in dense vegetation. They prefer cloudy water with a soft bottom. Warmouths can withstand low oxygen levels, high silt loads and temperatures into the 90s. Its small size keeps it off the radar of most fishermen, but it has a good flavor and is a scrappy, strong fighter on light tackle.

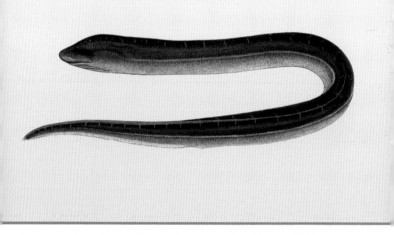

Description: dark olive or brown body with small dark spots, some spots light orange, pink or white; belly cream to light brown; body snake-like tapering to point; small eye; no paired fins; tiny tail fin; very slimy

Similar Species: American Eel (pg. 62)

Swamp Eel	American Eel	Swamp Eel	American Eel
no pectoral fins	pectoral fins	no dorsal or anal fin	continuous dorsal tail and anal fins

SWAMP EEL

Monopterus albus

Other Names: brown eel, swamp water snake

Habitat: slow-moving streams and canals; shallow lakes, ponds and swamps with dense vegetation and mud bottoms

Range: eastern and south Asia, Australia, established in Hawaii, Georgia and Florida; in Florida, the Little Manatee River and Bull Creek near Tampa, north Miami canals, the canals and swamps near Homestead

Food: small crustaceans, aquatic insects, tadpoles, worms and a few small fish

Reproduction: males build bubble nest that floats at the surface near the mouth of its burrows; males guards nest, eggs and young

Average Size: 1 to 2 feet, 8 ounces to 1 pound

Records: none

Notes: Swamp Eels were introduced into Hawaii in the early 1900s, into Georgia in 1994 and into Florida in 1997. They have not become a severe problem in Hawaii but have the potential to do a great deal of harm in Florida's swamps. Swamp Eels can breathe air and can migrate overland when forced by droughts or starvation. Swamp Eels are very secretive, spending the daylight hours in burrows dug in the mud. They are revered as food in Asia, but not often eaten in the U.S.

163

Description: gray-black back; silver sides with 6 to 8 uninterrupted black stripes; front of dorsal fin separated from soft-rayed rear portion; lower jaw protrudes beyond snout

Similar Species: Striped Bass (pg. 168)

White Bass	Striped Bass	White Bass	Striped Bass
stripes indistinct or missing	stripes distinct	one tooth patch on front of tongue, mouth protrudes beyond snout	two tooth patches on back of tongue

WHITE BASS

Morone chrysops

Other Names: lake, sand or silver bass, streaker

Habitat: large lakes, rivers and impoundments with relatively clear water

Range: Great Lakes region to the eastern seaboard, through the southeast to the Gulf and west to Texas; Apalachicola and Ochlockonee River systems in Florida's Panhandle

Food: small fish

Reproduction: spawns in late spring or early summer; eggs spread in open water over gravel beds or rubble 6 to 10 feet deep; some populations migrate to narrow bays or up tributary streams to spawn

Average Size: 9 to 18 inches, 8 ounces to 2 pounds

Records: State—4 pounds, 11 ounces, Apalachicola River, Gadsden County, 1992; North American—6 pounds, 13 ounces, Lake Orange, Virginia, 1989

Notes: White Bass inhabit the large river systems in Florida's Panhandle where they travel in large schools near the surface. They can often be spotted by watching for seagulls feeding on baitfish driven to the surface by schools of bass. In some areas, anglers gather in large numbers along streams during the spawning run. The flesh is somewhat soft, but has a good flavor and can be improved if it is put on ice and chilled as soon as it is caught.

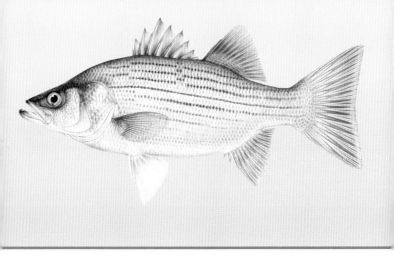

Description: dark gray back; bright silver sides with 7 or 8 broken stripes; dorsal fin separated, front has hard spines, rear has soft rays; two tooth patches, one on back of tongue

Similar Species: Striped Bass (pg. 168), White Bass (pg. 164)

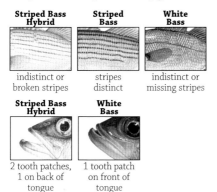

Striped Bass Hybrid	**Striped Bass**	**White Bass**
indistinct or broken stripes	stripes distinct	indistinct or missing stripes

Striped Bass Hybrid	**White Bass**
2 tooth patches, 1 on back of tongue	1 tooth patch on front of tongue

166

STRIPED BASS HYBRID

Morone saxatilis x Morone chrysops

Other Names: white striper, white rock, wiper, sunshine and Palmetto bass

Habitat: open water of large lakes and slow-moving rivers

Range: stocked in about 40 U.S. states; stocked from south central Florida north throughout the state

Food: small fish, insects, crustaceans

Reproduction: hatchery-produced hybrid that is only occasionally fertile

Average Size: 1 to 2 feet, 5 to 10 pounds

Records: State—16 pounds, 5 ounces, Lake Seminole, Jackson County, 1985; North American—27 pounds, 5 ounces, Greer's Ferry Lake, Arkansas, 1997

Notes: There are two Striped Bass Hybrids. The Sunshine Bass is a hatchery cross between a male Striped Bass and a female White Bass. The Palmetto Bass is the opposite, a cross between a male White Bass and a female Striped Bass. Both crosses are fertile but there is only limited reproduction. Florida now raises large numbers of these hybrids to stock in waters too warm to support Striped Bass. This hard-fighting, tasty hybrid bass has now become a favorite with anglers in Florida and across the country. The Hybrid Striped Bass is also becoming an important aquaculture fish, supplying fillets for the grocery and restaurant market.

Description: dark gray back; bright silver sides with 7 or 8 distinct stripes; jaw protrudes beyond snout; dorsal fin separated, front part hard spines, rear part soft rays

Similar Species: Striped Bass Hybrid (pg. 166), White Bass (pg. 164)

Striped Bass	**Striped Bass Hybrid**	**White Bass**
distinct stripes	indistinct or broken stripes	indistinct or missing stripes

Striped Bass	**Striped Bass Hybrid**	**White Bass**
two tooth patches one on back of tongue	two tooth patches one on back of tongue	one tooth patch on front of tongue

STRIPED BASS

Morone saxatilis

Moronidae

Other Names: striper, streaker, surf bass, rockfish

Habitat: coastal oceans and associated spawning streams; landlocked in some large lakes and reservoirs

Range: Atlantic coast from Maine to northern Florida, Gulf Coast from Florida to Texas, introduced to the Pacific coast and some large inland impoundments; in Florida, from the St. Johns River north in eastern Florida to the Panhandle rivers in western Florida

Food: small fish

Reproduction: spawns in late spring to early summer in freshwater streams; eggs deposited in riffles over gravel bars at the mouth of large tributaries; eggs must remain suspended to hatch

Average Size: 18 to 30 inches, 10 to 20 pounds

Records: State—42 pounds, 3 ounces, Apalachicola River, Gadsden County, 1993; North American—78 pounds, 8 ounces, Atlantic City, New Jersey, 1992

Notes: The Striped Bass is a saltwater fish that migrates into fresh water to spawn. Striped Bass are now reared in hatcheries and stocked in many large southern and western lakes and rivers. Most of these populations cannot reproduce naturally and must be maintained through stocking programs. Some of Florida's Striped Bass remain year-round in the larger rivers. They are large, hard-fighting sport fish and excellent table fare.

169

Description: olive to brown back; sides yellow-brown with dark lateral bands; slender fish with pelvic, dorsal and anal fins set well back on body; long snout flattened on top; rounded tail; upturned mouth

Similar Species: Brook Silverside (pg. 114)

Banded Killifish	Brook Silverside	Banded Killifish	Brook Silverside
single dorsal fin	two dorsal fins	rounded snout, large eye	pointed snout, small eye

Banded Killifish	Brook Silverside
finger-shaped protruding anal fin	long anal fin with straight or concave edge

BANDED KILLIFISH

Fudulus cingulatus

Other Names: barred minnow, freshwater mummichog, freshwater killy, banded topminnow

Habitat: still pools in slow-moving streams; shoal waters of large lakes and brackish estuaries

Range: Maritime Provinces of Canada south through the Carolinas, west to Idaho; in Florida, from the Panhandle to the Suwannee River

Food: insects and crustaceans

Reproduction: spawns when water temperature reaches the low 70s; female lays 1 to 30 eggs suspended on long filaments; eggs are fertilized while still attached to the female, then drop to bottom to hatch unattended

Average Size: 2 to 3 inches

Records: none

Notes: As the name implies, "topminnows" inhabit the upper water column and are adapted to feeding on or near the surface. Though inconspicuous and well camouflaged, they are the favorite target of wading birds. Banded Killifish can live both in marine and fresh water. They withstand low oxygen levels well and are often used as bait minnows and are farmed in Michigan for this purpose. Though not very colorful, they make good aquarium fish and readily eat food spread on the water's surface.

Description: A dusky brown to olive back; silver sides; zigzag black stripe from head to black spot at base of tail; breeding males have a blue dorsal and anal fin; slender fish with pelvic, dorsal and anal fins set well back on body; long snout flattened on top; rounded tail; upturned mouth

Similar Species: Brook Silverside (pg. 114)

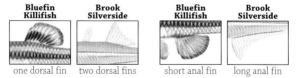

Bluefin Killifish	Brook Silverside	Bluefin Killifish	Brook Silverside
one dorsal fin	two dorsal fins	short anal fin	long anal fin

BLUEFIN KILLIFISH

Lucania goodei

Fundulidae

Other Names: spring killifish, blue fintop minnow

Habitat: shallow water of ponds, lakes, springs, and low gradient streams with backwaters, all with dense vegetation

Range: Florida and coastal Carolinas; in Florida, east of the Choctawhatchee River drainage

Food: algae and small pieces of higher plants

Reproduction: spawns throughout spring and summer in dense vegetation; female lays 1 to 30 eggs that attach to the vegetation to hatch unattended

Average Size: 2 to 3 inches

Records: none

Notes: The topminnow family is a group of fish that is adapted to living near the water's surface. They have large swim bladders to keep them floating high in the water column and upturned mouths for picking food from the surface. The Bluefin Killifish is somewhat of an exception, often staying well below the surface to feed on algae. Killifish and topminnows are well represented in Florida, with well over a dozen species present in the state. Bluefins are widespread in Florida and often associated with springs and spring brooks.

GLOSSARY

adipose fin a small, fleshy fin without rays, located on the midline of the fish's back between the dorsal fin and the tail

air bladder a balloon-like organ located in the gut area of a fish, used to control buoyancy—and in the respiration of some species such as gar; also called "swim bladder" or "gas bladder"

alevin a newly hatched fish that still has its yolk sac

anadromous a fish that hatches in freshwater, migrates to the ocean, then re-enters streams or rivers from the sea (or large inland body of water) to spawn

anal fin a single fin located on the underside near the tail

annulus marks or rings on the scales, spine, vertebrae or otoliths that scientists use to determine a fish's age

anterior toward the front of a fish, opposite of posterior

bands horizontal markings running lengthwise along the side of a fish

barbel thread-like sensory structures on a fish's head often near the mouth, commonly called "whiskers"; used for taste or smell

bars vertical markings on the side of a fish

benthic organisms living in or on the bottom of a body of water

brood swarm a large group or "cloud" of young fish such as Black Bullheads

carnivore a predatory fish that feeds on other fish (also called a piscivore) or animals

catadromous a fish that lives in freshwater and migrates into saltwater to spawn, such as the American Eel

caudal fin the tail or tail fin

caudal peduncle the portion of the fish's body located between the anal fin and the beginning of the tail

coldwater referring to a species or environment; in fish, often a species of trout or salmon found in water that rarely exceeds 70 degrees F; also used to describe a lake or river according to average summer temperature

copepod a small (less than 2 mm) crustacean, part of the zooplankton community

crustacean a crayfish, water flea, crab or other animal belonging to group of mostly aquatic species that have paired antennae, jointed legs and an exterior skeleton (exoskeleton); common food for many fish

dorsal relating to the top of the fish, on or near the back; opposite of the ventral, or lower, part of the fish

174

dorsal fin the fin or fins located along the top of a fish's back

eddy a circular water current, often created by an obstruction

epilimnion the warm, oxygen-rich upper layer of water in a thermally stratified lake

exotic a foreign species, not native to a watershed, such as the Zebra Mussel

fingerling a juvenile fish, generally 1 to 10 inches in length, in its first year of life

fork length the overall length of fish from mouth to the deepest part of the tail notch

fry recently hatched young fish that have already absorbed their yolk sacs

game fish a species regulated by laws for recreational fishing

gills organs used in aquatic respiration (breathing)

gill cover large bone covering the fish's gills, also called opercle or operculum

gill flap also called ear flap; fleshy projection on the back edge of the gill cover of some fish such as Bluegill

gill raker a comblike projection from the gill arch

harvest fish that are caught and kept by recreational or commercial anglers

hypolimnion bottom layer of the water column in a thermally stratified lake (common in summer); usually depleted of oxygen by decaying matter and inhospitable to most fish

ichthyologist a scientist who studies fish

invertebrates animals without backbones, such as insects, leeches and earthworms

kype hooked jaw acquired by some trout and salmon mainly during breeding season

lateral line a series of pored scales along the side of a fish that contain organs used to detect vibrations

littoral zone the part of a lake that is less than 15 feet in depth; this important and often vulnerable area holds the majority of aquatic plants, is a primary area used by young fish, and offers essential spawning habitat for most warmwater fishes such as Walleye and Largemouth Bass

mandible lower jaw

maxillary upper jaw

milt semen of a male fish that fertilizes the female's eggs during the spawning process

mollusk an invertebrate with a smooth, soft body such as a clam or a snail, often having an outer shell

native an indigenous or naturally occurring species

omnivore a fish or animal that eats plants and animal matter

opercle the bone covering the gills, also called the gill cover or operculum

otolith calcium concentration found in the inner ear of fish; used to determine age of some fish; also called ear bone

panfish small freshwater game fish that can be fried whole in a pan, such as Black Crappie, Bluegill and Yellow Perch

pectoral fins paired fins on the side of the fish located just behind the gills

pelagic fish species that live in open water, in the food-rich upper layer of the column; not associated with the bottom

pelvic fins paired fins located below or behind the pectoral fins on the bottom (ventral portion) of the fish

pheromone a chemical scent secreted as a means of communication between members of the same species

piscivore a predatory fish that mainly eats other fish

planktivore a fish that feeds on plankton

plankton floating or weakly swimming aquatic plants and animals, including larval fish, that drift with the current; often eaten by fish; individual organisms are called plankters

plankton bloom a marked increase in the amount of plankton due to favorable conditions such as nutrients and light

range the geographic region in which a species is found

ray, hard stiff fin support; resembles a spine but is jointed

ray, soft flexible fin support, sometimes branched

redd a nest-like depression made by a male or female fish during the spawn, often refers to nest of trout and salmon species

riprap rock or concrete used to protect a lakeshore or river's bank from erosion

roe fish eggs

scales small, flat plates covering the outer skin of many fish

Secchi disc an 8- to 12-inch-diameter, black-and-white circular disc used to measure water clarity; scientists record the average depth at which the disc disappears from sight when lowered into the water

silt small, easily disturbed bottom particles smaller than sand but larger than clay

siltation the accumulation of soil particles

spawning the process of fish reproduction; involves females laying eggs and males fertilizing them to produce young fish

spine stiff, non-jointed structures found along with soft rays in some fins

176

spiracle an opening on the posterior portion of the head above and behind the eye

standard length length of the fish from the mouth to the end of the vertebral column

stocking the purposeful, artificial introduction of a fish species into a body of water

substrate bottom composition of a lake, stream or river

subterminal mouth a mouth below the snout of the fish

swim bladder see air bladder

tailrace area of water immediately downstream of a dam or power plant

terminal mouth forward facing

thermocline middle layer of water in a stratified lake, typically oxygen rich, characterized by a sharp drop in temperature; often the lowest depth at which fish can be routinely found

total length length of fish from the mouth to the tail compressed to its fullest length

tributary a stream that feeds into another stream, river or lake

turbid cloudy; water clouded by suspended sediments or plant matter that limits visibility and the passage of light

velocity the speed of water flowing in a stream or river

vent the opening at the end of the digestive tract

ventral the underside of the fish

vertebrate an animal with a backbone

warmwater a non-salmonid species of fish that lives in water that routinely exceeds 70 degrees F; also used to describe a lake or river according to average summer temperature

yolk the part of an egg containing food for the developing fish

zooplankton the animal component of plankton; tiny animals that float or swim weakly; common food for small fish

INDEX

179

PRIMARY REFERENCES

Bass, G., Shafland, P. and Wattendorf, B
Freshwater Fishes of Florida
MyFWC.com
Florida Fish and Wildlife Conservation Commission, 2007

Danaway, Vic
Sport Fishes of Florida
Florida Sportsman, 2004

Jenkins, R. E. and Burkhead, N. M
Freshwater Fishes of Virginia
American Fisheries Society, 2007

Lee, D. S. et al.
Atlas of North American Freshwater Fishes
North Carolina State Museum of Natural History, 2007

McClane, A. J.
Freshwater Fishes of North America
Henry Holt and Company, 1978

Page, L. M. and Burr, B. M.
Freshwater Fishes, Peterson Field Guide
Houghton Mifflin Company, 1991

ABOUT THE AUTHOR

Dave Bosanko was born in Kansas and studied engineering before following his love of nature to degrees in biology and chemistry from Emporia State University. He spent thirty years as staff biologist at two of the University of Minnesota's field stations. Though his training was in mammal physiology, Dave worked on a wide range of research projects ranging from fish, bird and mammal population studies to experiments with biodiversity and prairie restoration. A lifelong fisherman and avid naturist, he is now spending his retirement writing, fishing and traveling.